11+
Maths
Success

11+ tests

Rob Kearsley-Bullen, Val Mitchell, Sally Moon

Contents

The 11+ tests are used by schools to find out about your thinking and learning skills and how you apply these to maths, comprehension (understanding), writing and problem solving.

You will be asked to take a selection of tests that could include some or all of the subjects listed on this page. There are a number of standardised tests schools can use, although some local authorities and schools write their own tests. This book guides you through the question styles, formats and levels of difficulty in the standardised tests, as well as providing examples of other question types that frequently occur.

Schools will often give you an interview in addition to the tests so that they can find out more about you. They may also set a problem-solving task.

Subjects set in the 11+ tests

Maths

The Maths paper will consist of a written test and probably a mental maths test in which the questions are read out to you. Calculators are not allowed in either test. Schools often write their own mental maths tests. The papers generally test the following skills.

Main test
- Numbers and their properties
- Calculations (including algebra)
- Fractions, decimals and percentages
- Working with charts and data
- Shape and space
- Measuring
- Data handling

Mental maths test

Verbal reasoning

Verbal reasoning tests ask you to solve puzzles and problems that involve letters, words and numbers and the connections between them.

Non-verbal reasoning

Non-verbal reasoning tests ask you to solve puzzles and problems that involve visual patterns or sequences and their connections.

English

The English paper will consist of a reading test and may also contain a separate writing task. There is no standardised form of writing task and schools often create their own. The papers are generally divided in the following ways.

Reading
- Comprehension
- Grammar
- Punctuation
- Spelling

Writing

Essential research

- Find out as much information as possible about your selected schools well in advance.
- You can find information on dates and entrance exams for state grammar schools on your local authority website or the school website.
- Individual schools include information in their prospectuses and additional information is often available on the school websites or at open days.
- Closing dates for applications vary, so you should check these well in advance.

11+ Maths Success is designed to help you prepare for the 11+ Maths paper in **five simple steps** so that you can take the tests with confidence.

The colour-coded sections in this guide split up the process, making it easy to follow.

1 Test   Find out what you know

Take Test 1 in the centre of the book and mark your answers. This will show what you already know and where you need to do more work.

2 Track   Plan your practice

Fill in the grids to target the specific skills you want to develop. This will help you to plan your work and decide how much time you need to set aside.

3 Teach   Improve your skills

Work through the Skills pages indicated by your grids and test yourself with the questions at the end of each section. All the answers are clearly explained to help you understand where you have gone wrong if you make any mistakes. Colour in the progress chart.

4 Test   Test for success

Take Test 2 in the centre of the book and mark your scores on the second set of grids to find out how you have improved.

Missed a few skills? Don't worry, just go back through any of the Skills pages you need to work on…

You can now move on to a full 11+ test, fully prepared. Look at the list of papers available on the inside front cover to see which is most suitable for you.

5 Present   Show what you can do

Practise your presentation skills using the interview tips and techniques on pages 86–87. If you are asked for an interview at the school you have chosen, this is your chance to shine.

The 11+ Maths tests are designed to test your basic knowledge of Maths and also to test how well you can solve problems with these skills.

You will probably be required to do two tests: one to find out about your **basic maths** skills and one to find out about your **mental maths** skills. Calculators are not allowed in either test. The Maths tests can include the following sections (although they may not be labelled).

Main maths test

Numbers and their properties
The skills covered
This section will include a range of questions that test your skills in place value, number patterns and sequences.

What you will have to do
You will be asked questions to see if you can…
- order and round whole numbers
- find and extend number patterns and sequences
- find factors and multiples.

Calculations
The skills covered
This section will include a range of questions that test your skills in addition, subtraction, multiplication and division. You will need to use pencil and paper methods as calculators are not generally allowed.

What you will have to do
You will be asked questions to see if you can…
- add and subtract whole numbers
- multiply and divide whole numbers
- solve problems involving the four operations, $+ - \times \div$
- work out basic problems involving algebra.

Fractions, decimals and percentages
The skills covered
This section will include a range of questions that test your skills in making connections between fractions, decimals and percentages. You may also be asked to solve problems where you will need to use your skills to investigate ratios and proportions.

What you will have to do
You will be asked questions to see if you understand…
- fractions
- decimals
- percentages
- how fractions, decimals and percentages are linked
- ratio and proportion.

Working with charts and data
The skills covered
This section will include a range of questions that test your skills in organising and interpreting information into charts, diagrams and graphs. You will also be expected to solve problems involving likely and unlikely outcomes.

What you will have to do
You will be questioned to see if you can…
- read and interpret charts and graphs
- find the mode, median, mean and range of a set of numbers
- understand probability.

The 11+ Maths tests

Shape and space

The skills covered

This section will include a range of questions that test whether you can sort shapes by their properties and calculate angles in a range of situations. You will also need to know the difference between area and perimeter, and be able to understand coordinates, and rotate and translate shapes.

What you will have to do

You will be asked questions to see if you can…

- understand the properties of 2-D and 3-D shapes
- measure and work out angles
- measure and work out perimeter, area and volume
- understand and work with coordinates
- understand and work with reflection, translation and rotation
- solve patterns and puzzles.

Measuring

The skills covered

This section will include a range of questions that test your knowledge of metric weights and measures as well as imperial measurements in common use. There may also be questions involving analogue and digital time (including the 24-hour clock).

What you will have to do

You will be asked questions to see if you can solve problems involving…

- length, capacity and weight
- time.

Mental maths test

What the test is about

Many schools also set a Mental maths test. These tests are designed to check if you can remember your addition, subtraction, multiplication and division facts quickly. They are also testing your *basic* knowledge in the subject areas you will have encountered in the main Maths test. A set amount of time is given to answer each question. The questions may be read out or pre-recorded.

SATs practice

The Maths SATs that you take at the end of Year 6 also contain a Maths assessment and a Mental maths assessment, so all the skills you learn in this book will help you to tackle those as well.

The question types are similar and the information in Chapter 3 *Improve your skills* covers many of the skills you will need for your SATs tests.

The **Glossary** (pages 76–79) will help you to understand the technical vocabulary in the Maths SATs papers. It contains important maths vocabulary you will have been taught in school and will be expected to know in these assessments. The terms are highlighted in bold.

INTERVIEWS

Schools often make their final selection by interviewing the candidates. This is where you get a chance to show your potential to be a good member of the school, and to find out whether this is the right place for you. Find out about more about interview techniques on pages 86–87.

How this book will help you

This book is designed to help you succeed in your 11+ Maths tests. After you have taken the first set of Practice tests, you will be directed to the appropriate *Improve your skills* pages in Chapter 3. After completing these pages, use the second set of more challenging Practice tests to check you are ready for the 11+ tests.

The final chapter in the book, *5 Show what you can do*, will help you to build your confidence as the 11+ tests approach and prepare you for the interview that many schools give.

Understanding the skills

After taking the first set of Practice tests, Chapter *3 Improve your skills* will...

- help you to understand how to answer questions about **place value**, **number patterns** and **sequences**
- show you methods for calculating **addition**, **subtraction**, **multiplication** and **division** and how to apply them to **algebra** problems
- help you to understand how to make connections between **fractions**, **decimals**, **percentages**, **ratios** and **proportions**
- show you how to organise and interpret information in **chart**, **diagram** and **graph form** and how to solve problems involving **probability**
- show you how to classify **2-D** and **3-D shapes** by their properties and calculate **angles** in a range of situations, work out areas and **perimeters**, understand **coordinates**, and **translate** and **rotate shapes**
- help you to understand metric and imperial **weights** and **measures** and solve questions involving **time**.

Practising the skills

To help you practise these skills as you work through the book, you will find...

- example questions and a short test in each section, providing extra practice
- 'Try it out' activities to build your skills
- a glossary of words that occur frequently in the tests.

Preparing for the tests

When your practice is complete, Chapter 5 Show what you can do on pages 84–87 can help you to relax and prepare yourself in the final week. It contains...

- a range of activities to do with your parents and friends to help you become more familiar with the skills you have learnt
- a 'countdown' list to help you get ready
- interview advice on how to dress, relax and communicate
- information about what happens after you get your 11+ test results.

Before you begin your 11+ practice, you need to work out how much you already know. As well as using this book, you may find it helpful to ask your school or your tutor about the skills you need to work on. The Internet is another useful source of information.

SATs (the Statutory Assessment Tests)

- You will have taken one in Year 2 and will take another at the end of Year 6.
- The average Level attained at Year 2 is Level 2; the average Level attained at Year 6 is Level 4.
- Your school may predict the level you will reach in Maths at the end of each Key Stage and you can ask for these records.

Teacher's assessment

Teachers assess your progress during the year in Maths. This assessment is often scored in thirds of a Level: 2c, 2b, 2a; 3c, 3b, 3a; 4c, 4b, 4a; 5c, 5b, 5a. An 'a' score is the highest in each Level. You should be working at Level 4a to Level 5 when you take your 11+ tests.

Tutors

If you are using an independent tutor or tuition school, they will have similar information to your own school. They may also have data on your Non-verbal reasoning and Verbal reasoning abilities.

Mental maths

The school may keep a record of your progress in Mental maths. Don't be afraid to ask your teacher for this information. Knowing how well you answer questions in a set time can help you plan your practice in key maths facts.

School

Your class teachers will have given you a number of tests during your time at school and they can give you helpful feedback about your progress in maths and mental maths.

Multiplication tables

- Knowing your multiplication tables (and the related division facts) helps you to solve many calculations quickly and identify patterns and sequences. It is important that you can answer multiplication and division questions in order, randomly and at speed.
- Check your knowledge of multiplication facts using this table. Work with an adult to see if you can…

  - say the table in order up to 12 times each number – tick the box if you can
  - answer 48 random questions – tick the box when you can answer all the questions correctly
  - answer 48 random questions in a minute – *write down the number you can reach every time you are tested to see how you improve.*

$\times$	Say in order	Answer 48 random questions	
		untimed	in one minute
1			
2			
3			
4			
5			
6			
7			
8			
9			
10			
11			
12			

Now you are ready to take the Practice tests, it is important to make sure you have the right conditions to get an accurate result.

These Practice tests (located in the pull-out booklet) will help you to identify the areas you will need to target for further practice.

Timing

It is better to do the tests in a morning at a weekend when you are at your best, rather than after school when you have had a long day.

Allow the following times for each test plus at least half an hour to get everything organised.

- Maths test 1: 45 minutes
- Mental maths test 1: about 15 minutes.

Equipment

You should have the following items assembled before you begin:

- pen   • pencil   • eraser
- pencil sharpener   • ruler
- timer (this can be the timer on an oven or an alarm clock)
- analogue watch/clock (as this will help you to see how much time you've got left)
- paper (for jotting ideas; your start and finish times)
- tracing paper
- a mirror to help with symmetry questions
- Mental maths answer sheet (this is on page 15 of the pull-out booklet).

Surroundings

You should use a clear table or desk so that you can set out the materials you will be using.

Make sure the area is quiet and without any distractions.

You will need to make sure somebody is available to help you with the Mental maths test. Someone will need to read out the questions to you so that you can write down your answers on the answer sheet (see page 15 of the pull-out booklet).

Question format
Multiple-choice

If you are taking a 'standardised' 11+ Maths test, this will be provided in a multiple-choice or standard format. Both formats use multiple-choice questions, although they are answered in slightly different ways. On the multiple-choice version, a separate answer grid is used and on the standard version the answers are written on the test paper.

Answers with letters

Many of the questions will have a list of letter options (usually A to E) for you to choose from. These letters are also printed in the answer grid when one is provided, and you simply mark the answer against the letter as instructed. You will find a lot of questions laid out in this style in the Maths tests in this book.

Answers without letters

A number of other questions in the standardised tests (where an answer grid is supplied) do not have letter options to choose from. Do not make the mistake of writing the answer on the test paper as there will be a list of answers to choose from in the answer grid.

Written format

When local authorities, schools and examination boards set their own papers, some or all of the questions are likely to be in a written format. For these questions, you will not be given any options to choose from. You will find some of these question types in the Maths tests in this book.

TIPS FOR SUCCESS

- Read each question twice.
- Don't guess any answers even if you are short of time. These tests are to help you find out areas where you need practice.

Once you have completed the Practice tests in the pull-out booklet, you will be ready to mark them. Do this by following the stages below.

Marking

Maths test

- Go to the *Answers* on page 91. Score your completed paper by filling in the blank boxes in the 'Mark column'. There is one mark allowed for each complete question – **there are no half marks**.
- Now turn to *Maths grid 1* on page 14.
- Transfer your marks to the 'Mark*' column.
- Add up the total for each section.
- Add up the total for all the sections in the final box at the end of the Maths grid.
- Work out the percentage as directed in the Summary box on page 12.

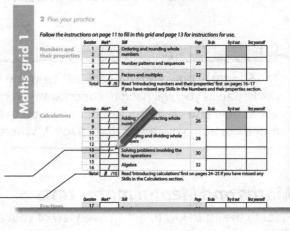

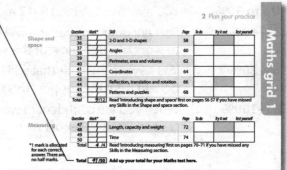

Mental maths test

- Go to the *Answers* on page 93. Score your completed paper by filling in the blank boxes in the 'Mark column'. There is one mark allowed for each complete question – **there are no half marks**.
- Now turn to *Mental maths grid 1* on page 15.
- Transfer your marks to the 'Mark*' column.
- Add up the total.
- Work out the percentage as directed in the Summary box on page 12.

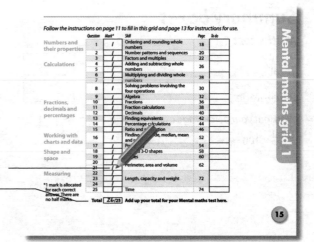

Summarising the tests

Now that you have all your results from the first Practice tests, you can begin to plan your time to work on the skills you may need to practise.

Understanding the summary boxes

The Summary boxes on this page will help you to build an overview of the key areas you will need to concentrate on in your 11+ practice. You should also view your results in relation to the information you found out from your research on page 9, 'Where you are now'.

Maths and Mental maths tests

Refer to the list below to get an overview of your abilities in *maths* and *mental maths*.

Up to 50%	You may need to plan 9–12 months of practice before attempting the 11+.
51–60%	Feel encouraged that you will benefit from this book, although you may need to work through most of the skills pages.
61–80%	You have many skills that will help you in your 11+ tests already and will benefit from the support this book will give you.
81–100%	When you are confident in working with the targeted skills, move on to the second (harder) set of Practice tests in the pull-out booklet.

Summary boxes

Maths test 1

Total

Percentage

Work out your percentage using this sum

$\frac{Total}{50} \times 100 =$

Mental maths test 1

Total

Percentage

Work out your percentage using this sum

$\frac{Total}{25} \times 100 =$

Understanding the grids

Maths grid

Maths grid 1 on page 14 (where you have marked your scores for Maths test 1) is an essential tool in planning your 11+ practice.

Turn to the grid and look at the 'To do' column. You will see that questions are grouped into blocks.

- Colour the blocks in **green** where you have answered **all** the questions **right.**
- Colour the blocks in **red** where you have answered **some or all** of the questions **wrong.**

Red sections

Look at the sections (Numbers and their properties; Calculations; Fractions, decimals and percentages; Working with charts and data; Shape and space and Measuring) where you have coloured blocks in red. Begin by looking at the relevant Introductions to these sections in Chapter *3 Improve your skills* (the page numbers are written next to the headings). For example, if you have coloured 'Ordering and rounding whole numbers' in red, then you should begin by reading *'Introducing numbers and their properties'* on page 16. Now work through the rest of the section in *3 Improve your skills* to complete the skills you marked in red earlier…

- Read through the text.
- Have a go at the 'Try it out' activities.
- Complete the questions at the end (and check your answers on pages 89–90).
- When you have finished the skill, colour in the 'Try it out' and 'Test yourself' boxes on Maths grid 1. Some skills do not have 'Try it out' activities and these blocks are coloured in grey on the grid.

Make a note of any questions you found difficult so that you can go back to these pages again before you take the 11+ test.

Green sections

If you have coloured any blocks in green, you have already mastered some of the easier skills needed in these sections, so you may not want to go through them as thoroughly. However, skimming quickly through the pages and trying out some activities will provide you with some tips to help you to speed up your test technique and tackle more difficult questions.

Working through the questions on these pages will also help to build your confidence in areas that you enjoy.

	Page	To do	Try it out	Test yourself
...ding and subtracting whole ...mbers	26			
...ltiplying and dividing whole ...mbers	28			
...ving problems involving the ...r operations	30			
...ebra	32			

...d 'Introducing calculations' first on pages 24–25 if you have missed any ...ls in the Calculations section.

Mental maths grid

The Mental maths grid 1 on page 15 (where you have marked your scores for Mental maths test 1) is a helpful additional tool to Maths grid 1 as it shows how quickly and accurately you can remember facts and solve problems.

Turn to the grid and look at the 'To do' column.

The questions are grouped in blocks in the same way as they are for Maths grid 1 (although not all of the skills are covered here).

- Colour the blocks in **green** where you have answered **all** the questions **right.**
- Colour the blocks in **red** where you have answered **some or all** of the questions **wrong**.

It is likely that the skills you have highlighted in red will link to the skills you have highlighted in Maths grid 1. Compare the two grids and make a note on the *Maths grid* of any sections where you may need additional practice.

If your percentage score is higher on the Mental maths test than the Maths test, you may need practice in reading the questions carefully. If your percentage score is higher on the Maths test than the Mental maths test, you may need practice in recalling your maths facts at speed.

...estion	Mark*	Skill	Page	To do
1		Ordering and rounding whole numbers	18	
2		Number patterns and sequences	20	
3		Factors and multiples	22	
4		Adding and subtracting whole numbers	26	
5				
6		Multiplying and dividing whole numbers	28	
7				
8		Solving problems involving the	30	

Maths grid 1

Follow the instructions on page 11 to fill in this grid and page 13 for instructions for use.

Numbers and their properties

Question	Mark*	Skill	Page	To do	Try it out	Test yourself
1		Ordering and rounding whole numbers	18			
2						
3		Number patterns and sequences	20			
4						
5		Factors and multiples	22			
6						
Total	/6	Read 'Introducing numbers and their properties' first on pages 16–17 if you have missed any Skills in the Numbers and their properties section.				

Calculations

Question	Mark*	Skill	Page	To do	Try it out	Test yourself
7		Adding and subtracting whole numbers	26			
8						
9						
10		Multiplying and dividing whole numbers	28			
11						
12						
13		Solving problems involving the four operations	30			
14						
15		Algebra	32			
16						
Total	/10	Read 'Introducing calculations' first on pages 24–25 if you have missed any Skills in the Calculations section.				

Fractions, decimals and percentages

Question	Mark*	Skill	Page	To do	Try it out	Test yourself
17		Fractions	36			
18						
19		Fraction calculations	38			
20						
21		Decimals	40			
22						
23		Finding equivalents	42			
24						
25		Percentage calculations	44			
26						
27		Ratio and proportion	46			
28						
Total	/12	Read 'Introducing fractions, decimals and percentages' first on pages 34–35 if you have missed any Skills in the Fractions, decimals and percentages section.				

Working with charts and data

Question	Mark*	Skill	Page	To do	Try it out	Test yourself
29		Charts and graphs	50			
30						
31		Finding the mode, median, mean and range	52			
32						
33		Probabilty	54			
34						
Total	/6	Read 'Introducing working with charts and data' first on pages 48–49 if you have missed any Skills in the Working with charts and data section.				

Shape and space

Question	Mark*	Skill	Page	To do	Try it out	Test yourself
35		2-D and 3-D shapes	58		▓	
36						
37		Angles	60			
38						
39		Perimeter, area and volume	62			
40						
41		Coordinates	64			
42						
43		Reflection, translation and rotation	66		▓	
44						
45		Patterns and puzzles	68			
46						
Total	/12	Read 'Introducing shape and space' first on pages 56-57 if you have missed any Skills in the Shape and space section.				

Measuring

Question	Mark*	Skill	Page	To do	Try it out	Test yourself
47		Length, capacity and weight	72		▓	
48						
49		Time	74			
50						
Total	/4	Read 'Introducing measuring' first on pages 70–71 if you have missed any Skills in the Measuring section.				

*1 mark is allocated for each correct answer. There are no half marks.

Total [/50] **Add up your total for your Maths test here.**

Follow the instructions on page 11 to fill in this grid and page 13 for instructions for use.

	Question	Mark*	Skill	Page	To do
Numbers and their properties	1		Ordering and rounding whole numbers	18	
	2		Number patterns and sequences	20	
	3		Factors and multiples	22	
Calculations	4		Adding and subtracting whole numbers	26	
	5				
	6		Multiplying and dividing whole numbers	28	
	7				
	8		Solving problems involving the four operations	30	
	9		Algebra	32	
Fractions, decimals and percentages	10		Fractions	36	
	11		Fraction calculations	38	
	12		Decimals	40	
	13		Finding equivalents	42	
	14		Percentage calculations	44	
	15		Ratio and proportion	46	
Working with charts and data	16		Finding the mode, median, mean and range	52	
	17		Probabilty	54	
Shape and space	18		2-D and 3-D shapes	58	
	19		Angles	60	
	20		Perimeter, area and volume	62	
	21				
Measuring	22		Length, capacity and weight	72	
	23				
	24				
	25		Time	74	

*1 mark is allocated for each correct answer. There are no half marks.

Total [/25] **Add up your total for your Mental maths test here.**

Introducing numbers and their properties

From counting objects to carrying out complex calculations, a knowledge of numbers and their properties underpins all of Maths. A number question gives you the chance to show that you understand what the different types of number are and how to use them correctly.

Knowing the properties of a number allows you to understand its relationships to other numbers and can help you calculate more efficiently.

What to expect

In the test, there will be questions about numbers and their properties, but you will also need to make use of these properties to answer questions from other parts of Maths. For example, knowing the factors of 60 is useful when you are trying to work out fractions of an hour.

Some questions in the test papers may be multiple-choice. To answer them, you need to select the correct number from the choices given. Sometimes the answers may be a set of two or three numbers with a particular property.

Number skills

Some of the properties of numbers that you need to learn are about the decimal place value system. Others are about the numbers themselves. For example, prime numbers are prime numbers, regardless of what system you use to write them down. 7 was a prime number to the Romans, even though they wrote it 'VII'.

1 You need to know the decimal place value system well.

We write the digits 0 to 9 in a series of places (or 'columns'), which means we can write numbers of any size we like with just ten symbols.

Each new position represents an increase in size of 10 times.

millions	hundred thousands	ten thousands	thousands	hundreds	tens	units or ones
	2	8	7	5	0	5

The number shown, 287 505, would be read as 'two hundred and eighty-seven thousand, five hundred and five'.

2 The most common use of negative numbers is to represent cold temperatures. It is quite usual for temperatures to dip to -3°C, -5°C, or even -10°C in winter.

The more negative a number gets, the lower it is. So -10°C is colder than -5°C.

Look at the number line on page 18 to help you understand this.

Introducing numbers and their properties

3 You often use rounded numbers when you want to estimate (get a rough idea of) the answer to a calculation.

To get a rough idea of the cost of 195 lunches costing £1.80 each, calculate 200 × £2 = £400

This isn't exactly right, but gives you a good idea of what the cost would be.

In the test, you will be expected to answer questions like these.

● Which description matches the numbers shown in the cloud?

A factors of 50

B multiples of 5 that are factors of 100

C square numbers and multiples of 5

D the next number is 200

E 100 divided by a single digit number

A 100 is not a factor of 50.

B All the numbers fit this description.

C 5, 10 and 50 are not square numbers.

D There isn't a sensible sequence here, even if you arrange the numbers in order of size.

E You have to divide 100 by 2-digit numbers to get 10 or 5.

So **B** *is the correct answer.*

● What number is missing from this sequence?

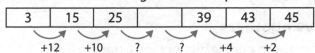

| 3 | 15 | 25 | | 39 | 43 | 45 |

+12   +10   ?   ?   +4   +2

*3 + **12** = 15 and 15 + **10** = 25*

*39 + **4** = 43 and 43 + **2** = 45*

*This suggests that the difference between numbers is decreasing by 2 each time. Test this out: 25 + **8** = 33 and 33 + **6** = 39*

The idea was correct. The missing number is 33.

TIPS FOR SUCCESS

Know those tables!

● Although this section isn't about calculations, seeing and understanding the connections between numbers is much easier if you are really familiar with the multiplication tables.
For example, if you want to pick out the multiples of 7 from a group of numbers, it will be a lot quicker if you know the 7 times table well.

Example: Which of these are multiples of 7?

15	**21**	64	**56**	**35**	43	54
no	*3 × 7*	*no*	*8 × 7*	*5 × 7*	*no*	*no*

What you will learn

In this section you will learn about these number topics:

● ordering whole numbers

● rounding whole numbers

● number patterns and sequences

● factors and multiples.

Ordering and rounding whole numbers

Whenever you compare the sizes of numbers, you are putting them in order. You can round numbers when you only need a rough idea of their size.

To compare the sizes of whole numbers (or **integers**), you need a good knowledge of the **decimal place value system** that we use. Sets of numbers may be put into **ascending order** (smallest to largest) or **descending order** (largest to smallest).

Understanding ordering

These words or phrases are clues that a question involves ordering:

order sort ascending descending biggest

smallest greatest least rank

…if you want to find out which are the most popular music downloads you can look at a list of download sales and 'rank' them in the 'order' of sales figures.

This number line shows **positive** and **negative numbers** near 0.

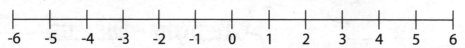

The further to the left a number appears on the line, the smaller it is. The further to the right, the larger it is. So although 5 is greater than 3, -3 is greater than -5.

Ordering skills

Sorting a set of positive numbers

When ordering whole numbers, the first thing to look at is how many digits each number has. For example, a number with five digits is bigger than a number with four digits. So these numbers are in ascending order:

950 3314 10289

Once you have grouped your numbers according to how many digits they have, you can work with each group. Look at all the numbers with the most digits. You can then order them by looking at their first digits. If any have the same first digit, look at the second digit, and so on. So these numbers are in descending order:

7743 7734 7077 6950

Sorting positive and negative numbers

To sort positive and negative numbers you can put the numbers on a number line. For example, put these numbers into order:

43 176 -85 -12 7

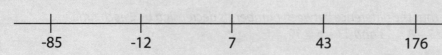

Rounding skills

Rounding to the nearest ten

To round to the nearest ten you need to find the **multiples** of ten on either side of your number. Suppose you want to round 643 to the nearest ten. 643 is 'sandwiched' between two multiples of ten: 640 and 650. It is closer to 640, so 643 to the nearest ten is 640.

Rounding to the nearest hundred or thousand

To round to the nearest hundred or thousand use the same idea as for rounding to the nearest ten. For example, to round 3684 to the nearest hundred, you need to see if it is closer to 3600 or 3700. The tens digit is 8, so it is closer to 3700. To round to the nearest thousand, look at 3000 and 4000. The hundreds digit is 6, so it is closer to 4000.

What if it's halfway?

You might want to round a number that is halfway between two tens, hundreds or thousands. Suppose you wanted to round 1585 to the nearest ten. 1585 is exactly halfway between 1580 and 1590. The rule is that if this happens, you *round up*, to 1590.

Solving problems with ordering and rounding

1 Use the rounding techniques to answer this question. Below are the mileages of three second-hand cars.

- Round the figures to the nearest thousand miles.

Car A 45 235   **Car B** 7500   **Car C** 106 664

Car A's mileage is between 45 000 and 46 000. The hundreds digit is 2, so round down, to 45 000.

Car B's mileage is between 7000 and 8000. The hundreds digit is 5, so round up, to 8000.

Car C's mileage is between 106 000 and 107 000. The hundreds digit is 6, so round up, to 107 000.

2 Use the sorting techniques to order the numbers.

- Write the heights of these English mountains in descending order.

Skiddaw 3054 feet   **Scafell Pike** 3208 feet   **Cross Fell** 2929 feet

All the heights have four digits. Look at the first digit; Skiddaw and Scafell Pike have a 3 in the thousands, but Cross Fell only has a 2, so it will come last. Now look at the hundreds; Skiddaw has a 0, Scafell Pike has a 2, so it is taller. So the order is Scafell Pike, Skiddaw, Cross Fell.

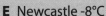

Understanding rounding

If the word 'rounding' isn't used in a question, these words or phrases are clues that the question involves rounding:

nearest ten/hundred/thousand

sensible   accuracy   rough(ly)

…if you are asked to estimate the number of people in a football ground, you will know that the person does not expect an exact answer but an answer to the nearest ten, hundred or thousand depending on the size of the ground.

TEST YOURSELF

1 The price of a house is £224 945. What is this rounded to:

  a the nearest ten

  b the nearest thousand

  c the nearest hundred thousand?

2 Which of these cities is the coldest?

  A Birmingham 0°C   **B** Exeter 8°C

  C Leeds -3°C   **D** London 5°C

  E Newcastle -8°C

Number patterns and sequences

A sequence is a chain of numbers linked by a mathematical rule. There are some common sets of numbers that you should be able to recognise. These are often called number patterns.

Usually the **rule** for a **sequence** will tell you what to do with the last number to find the next one; whether to add or subtract something, or even multiply or divide. For example, the sequence 5, 8, 11, 14… uses the rule 'add 3 to the last number'. The sequence 3, 6, 12, 24… uses the rule 'double the last number'.

Understanding number patterns

These are common number patterns that you should be able to recognise:

even numbers   **2, 4, 6, 8, 10, 12, 14, 16, 18, 20…**

Rule: start at 2, then add 2 to the last number to find the next term.

odd numbers   **1, 3, 5, 7, 9, 11, 13, 15, 17, 19…**

Rule: start at 1, then add 2 to the last number to find the next term.

square numbers   **1, 4, 9, 16, 25, 36, 49, 64, 81, 100…**

Rule: the squares of 1, 2, 3… 1 × 1, 2 × 2, 3 × 3, etc.

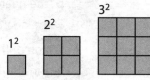

cube numbers   **1, 8, 27, 64, 125, 216, 343, 512, 729, 1000…**

Rule: the cubes of 1, 2, 3… 1 × 1 × 1, 2 × 2 × 2, 3 × 3 × 3, etc.

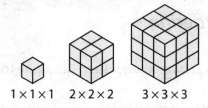

$1 \times 1 \times 1 \quad 2 \times 2 \times 2 \quad 3 \times 3 \times 3$

triangular numbers   **1, 3, 6, 10, 15, 21, 28, 36, 45, 55…**

Rule: start at 1, then add 2, 3, 4, 5…

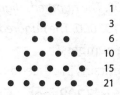

prime numbers   **2, 3, 5, 7, 11, 13, 17, 19, 23, 29…**

There is no rule for these – you just have to know them! (See page 22.)

Number pattern and sequence skills

Missing numbers and next numbers

Always check the differences between **consecutive numbers** in the sequence first. This will often reveal the rule. For example, to find the next number in the sequence **3, 7, 13, 21, 31**, you can see that you add 4, 6, 8, and 10. So add 12 to find the next number: $31 + 12 = $ **43**

Identifying numbers

You may be given a list of numbers and asked to identify one of them using some instructions. For example, which number in the list **16, 21, 25, 28, 36, 45, 49** is both **triangular** and **square**? All the numbers are either triangular or square, but only **36** is both.

See also the section on **common multiples** on page 22.

Solving problems with number patterns and sequences

1 Use lists to help you solve this problem.

- Write down a number that is a **multiple** of 5 and also a triangular number.

  Write a list of multiples of five: 5, 10, 15, 20, 25, 30…

  You can always add more numbers if there aren't enough. Write a list of triangular numbers: 1, 3, 6, 10, 15…

  You could actually have stopped at 10. You could give 10 or 15 as the answer.

2 Examine the differences between numbers to answer this question.

- Find the next number in this sequence: 6, 8, 7, 11, 10, 16, 15…

  The differences are:

6		8		7		11		10		16		15		?
	+2		-1		+4		-1		+6		-1				

  Every other difference is – 1, and the others increase by 2 each time, so you need to add 8 to find the next number → $15 + 8 = 23$

TRY IT OUT

Out and about

Whenever you are on a journey, look at road signs, car number plates, etc. Try to find something special about any numbers that you see.

- A road sign showing 'Manchester – 125 miles' would mean you'd found a cube number.

- The car number plate AB61 7YZ contains two prime numbers.

TEST YOURSELF

1 Which of these numbers is both triangular and prime?

2   6   10   3   13   21   23

2 Find the next number in this sequence:

5,   9,   17,   33,   65,   129…

3 Which row of the table contains a square, prime and cube number in that order?

A	7	4	9
B	16	23	8
C	9	31	15
D	11	16	27
E	25	12	1

Factors and multiples are part of the way different numbers are connected together by multiplication and division.

To recognise **factors** and **multiples**, it is important to know the **number bonds** for multiplication – in other words, the multiplication tables. The more multiplication facts you know, the faster you will be able to complete questions involving factors and multiples.

Understanding factors and multiples

The factors of a number are all the numbers that it divides by exactly, without leaving a **remainder**.

Factors always occur in *pairs* that multiply to give the original number.	The factors of 12 are 1, 2, 3, 4, 6 and 12, in three pairs: $1 \times 12 = 12$, $2 \times 6 = 12$ and $3 \times 4 = 12$
If the number is a **square number**, a factor will pair up with itself.	The factors of 25 are 1, 5 and 25, paired like this: $1 \times 25 = 25$ and $5 \times 5 = 25$
If a number has only two factors, it is **prime**.	The factors of 7 are 1 and 7: $1 \times 7 = 7$

The multiples of a number are what you get when you multiply it by 1, 2, 3, 4, 5…

Multiples of 2	2, 4, 6, 8, 10, 12, 14, 16, 18, 20…
Multiples of 7	7, 14, 21, 28, 35, 42, 49, 56, 63, 70…
Multiples of 15	15, 30, 45, 60, 75, 90, 105, 120, 135, 150…

…*so whenever you multiply numbers together, you are using your knowledge of multiples.*

Factor and multiple skills

Common factors

If two numbers have some factors that are the same, these are their **common factors**. For example:

the factors of 30 are 1, 2, 3, 5, 6, 10, 15, 30

the factors of 18 are 1, 2, 3, 6, 9, 18

The common factors of 18 and 30 are 1, 2, 3, 6, and the largest of these is 6, the **highest common factor** (HCF).

Common multiples

If you write out lists of the multiples of two different numbers, you may find some numbers that appear in both lists. These are the **common multiples** of the two numbers.

For example:

the multiples of 18 are 18, 36, 54, 72, 90, 108, 126, 144, 162, 180…

the multiples of 30 are 30, 60, 90, 120, 150, 180, 210, 240, 270, 300…

90 and 180 occur in both lists. 90 is the smallest, so it is the **lowest (or least) common multiple** (LCM) of 18 and 30. In fact, all the common multiples are multiples of the LCM, and if you carried on the lists far enough, you would find that 270, 360, 450… all appeared in both lists.

You use the LCM as the **lowest (or least) common denominator** for adding or subtracting **fractions** (see page 37).

Solving problems with factors and multiples

1 You need to have a logical way of working through the possible answers in this question.

- Which of these lists contains only factors of 15 or 16?

| **A** 4 5 6 | **B** 1 8 9 | **C** 8 10 15 | **D** 3 4 5 | **E** 1 2 6 |

Work through all the numbers, underlining all the factors of 16. Then work through them again, underlining all the factors of 15. There should be one list with all its numbers underlined. This one is the answer.

| **A** <u>4</u> <u>5</u> 6 | **B** <u>1</u> <u>8</u> 9 | **C** <u>8</u> 10 <u>15</u> | **D** <u>3</u> <u>4</u> <u>5</u> | **E** <u>1</u> <u>2</u> 6 |

*The answer is list **D**.*

2 To answer this question you need to realise that it is about common multiples.

- Callum puts coins weighing 12 grams each on one pan of a pair of scales.

  Amy puts coins weighing 10 grams each on the other pan.

  What is the smallest weight they can put on their scale pans so the scales balance?

  The weights Callum can put on his side are 12, 24, 36, 48, 60, 72…

  The weights Amy can put on her side are 10, 20, 30, 40, 50, 60…

  60 is the LCM of 12 and 10, so the answer is 60 grams.

TRY IT OUT

Dicey pairs

Roll two dice and multiply the two scores together. Write down the result. Now do it again to get another number. Make a list of the factors and multiples of your two numbers. Find the common factors and common multiples, the HCF and LCM.

You can also try it with three numbers, or use more dice. Or you can devise your own rules for making the starting numbers.

TEST YOURSELF

1 Which of these lists contains only multiples of 4 or 5?

| **A** 12 14 15 | **B** 8 12 13 | **C** 8 9 10 | **D** 8 10 11 | **E** 12 15 16 |

2 How many factors of 36 are also square numbers?

3 One lighthouse flashes every 45 seconds. Another flashes every 50 seconds. If they flash together at exactly 9pm how many seconds will pass before they flash together again?

Calculations are the way in which we process numbers to work out things that are useful to us. A calculation question gives you the chance to show that you can select the right mathematical operations to work out an answer, and then carry them out without making a mistake.

Being able to calculate successfully involves knowing a number of basic facts called number bonds. These are the results of small, simple calculations that you memorise and use as part of more complex calculations.

What to expect

In the test, there will be some questions that are just straightforward calculations built from numbers and operations, such as $(12 + 5) \times (10 - 3)$. However, most of the calculations that you do will probably be part of a context. This means that you will be given a problem to solve, and a calculation is required to find the answer. The real skill is in being able to process the information you are given in the right way.

Calculations can be performed on all sorts of quantities: frequencies, measurements, times – anything that can be written as a number.

Some questions in the test papers may be multiple-choice. To answer them you need to select the correct answer from the choices given. Sometimes the answer choices may be calculations themselves. For example, you may be asked to identify which of a list of calculations does *not* give the answer 10.

Calculation skills

The number bonds you use to carry out calculations include:
- being able to add and subtract single-digit numbers
- knowing complements (such as what has to be added to a number to make 100)
- using multiplication tables
- knowing the corresponding division facts.

1   You should always aim to be as efficient as possible when calculating.

You may have to use a formal 'column' method to do some calculations, but if you can think of a quicker shortcut, you should use it, as you have a lot of questions to do in the time you have available.

To multiply a number by 9, multiply by 10, then subtract the original number.

9 × a number + 1 × the number = 10 × the number.

2 Every mathematical operation has an opposite or *inverse*. You need to know how to apply these, as 'working backwards' is often the key to solving a problem.

Operation	+ 2	– 10	× 8	÷ 3	square (²)
Inverse	– 2	+ 10	÷ 8	× 3	square root (√)

This is particularly useful when you are solving an equation.

3 When operations are mixed together in the same calculation, they follow a set order, unless brackets 'interfere' with this. You may have learned this set order as **BIDMAS**:

- **B**rackets first
- then **I**ndices (powers)
- then **D**ivision and **M**ultiplication
- then **A**ddition and **S**ubtraction.

A good example of a mixed operation procedure is finding the *mean* of a set of numbers.

You need to find the total of the numbers, then divide this by how many numbers there are.

4 You need to understand algebraic notation. In particular, the way you write multiplication and division in algebra is a little different from how you write them when you are working just with numbers.

2x means '2 times x'

$\frac{a}{b}$ *means 'a divided by b'*

You may be asked to write an algebraic expression or formula that describes a situation given in words.

In the test, you can expect to find questions like these.

- Which of these calculations has an answer that is a square number?

  A 25 × 17 **B** 250 + 75 **C** 5^3

  D 361 – 136 **E** 1050 ÷ 2

  The answers are 425, 325, 125, 225 and 525.

  $225 = 15^2$, *so answer D is correct.*

- Add brackets to this calculation to make it correct.

  12 × 3 + 2 ÷ 4 + 1 = 16

  The answer is 12 × (3 + 2) ÷ 4 + 1 = 12 × 5 ÷ 4 + 1 = 60 ÷ 4 + 1 = 15 + 1 = 16

TIPS FOR SUCCESS

Number gym

- A good way to improve your calculation skills is to extend what you already know.

  Know your tables up to 10 × 10? Learn them up to 12 × 12

  Make sure you can reverse all your table facts. 6 × 8 = 48, so you should know (without thinking) that 48 ÷ 8 = 6 and 48 ÷ 6 = 8

  Know the squares up to 144? Learn them up to 400.

What you will learn

In this section you will learn about these calculation topics:

- adding and subtracting whole numbers
- multiplying and dividing whole numbers
- powers and square roots
- the order of operations
- solving problems involving mixed operations
- algebra.

Adding and subtracting whole numbers

Addition and subtraction are the first mathematical operations you learn about. You will know a number of different ways of tackling calculations like these; the trick is to know which to use for what.

To use any of the methods, you need a set of facts you can recall instantly, called **number bonds**. For example, you need to know that 5 + 7 = 12; if you didn't, you would have to count on from 5 every time you wanted to use this fact!

Understanding addition and subtraction

The following words or phrases are clues that a question will involve addition:

total   sum   altogether   perimeter

...if you are adding up the cost of two music downloads, you would add one to the other to see how much they cost 'altogether'.

These words or phrases are clues that a question will involve **subtraction**:

**difference   how many more (or less)   remains (or left)
change   a number missing from a table**

...if you wanted to find out how much of your £10 pocket money you had left after buying the downloads, you would subtract the cost from the £10 to find out the 'change'.

Addition and subtraction skills

Using number bonds

You can use number bonds as the starting point for all sorts of calculations. For example, if you know that 5 + 7 = 12, you immediately know that 12 − 5 = 7 and 12 − 7 = 5.

Speed and accuracy

If you need to add a number that is 'almost a **multiple** of 10', like 29 or 99, *add the multiple of 10 first*, then subtract 1. To subtract a number like this, subtract the multiple, then add 1. This method works well with numbers ending in 8, 7 or even 5 and is often quicker than using column addition.

When adding mentally, it is often easier to add a *smaller* number on to a *larger* number. For example, 28 + 4 is easier to add than 4 + 28.

When you need to add together a set of 3- or 4-digit numbers, you may find it easier to add the thousands, hundreds, tens and units separately. For example, you could calculate 1369 + 2217 + 1119 as follows: 4000 + 600 + 80 + 25

Negative numbers

To add a **negative number**, just subtract the **equivalent** positive number.
For example, 12 + (-7) = 12 − 7 = 5

You can also use a number line to help. This one shows 3 + (-8) = 3 − 8 = -5

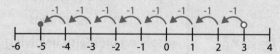

To subtract a negative number, just add the equivalent **positive number**.
For example, 7 − (-3) = 7 + 3 = 10

Solving problems with addition and subtraction

1 Look for the clues in this problem to see whether it is an addition or subtraction question.

- Over a bank holiday weekend, Jim sold the following numbers of ice-creams from his stall:

Saturday	Sunday	Monday
152	**188**	**79**

- How many did he sell altogether over the weekend?

'Altogether' is a hint that you need to add the three numbers together.

You could use a column method like this.

```
    ¯ 1  5  2          1  5  2          1  5  2
  +   1  8  8       +  1  8  8       +  1  8  8
  +      7  9       +     7  9       +     7  9
  _____       _____       _____
             9              1  9       4  1  9
  _____          _____       _____
       1                2  1             2  1
```

2 + 8 + 9 = 19, so write 9 in the units and carry 1.

5 + 8 + 7 + 1 = 21, so write 1 in the tens and carry 2.

1 + 1 + 2 = 4, so write 4 in the hundreds. Finished!

Alternatively, you could adjust the numbers so that you can calculate with simple jottings.

Subtract 2 from the first number and add 2 to the second:
152 + 188 = 150 + 190 = 340

Now 79 is 1 less than 80, so add 80 and subtract 1.
340 + 80 = 420   420 – 1 = 419

2 You can answer the following question using addition or subtraction:

- A coach journey is 255km long. The driver makes a rest stop after 169km. How far from the destination is this?

You could use a column method to subtract the distance travelled so far from the total length of the journey.

```
  1   4  15          1  14  4  15        1  14  4  15
  2̶   5̶   5̶          2̶   5̶   5̶           2̶   5̶   5̶
 -    1  6  9       -   1  6  9         -   1  6  9
  _____        _____         _____
             6              8  6              8  6
```

You can't take 9 from 5, so borrow 10 units. 15 – 9 = 6, so write 6 in the units.

You can't take 6 from 4, so borrow 10 tens. 14 – 6 = 8, so write 8 in the tens.

1 – 1 = 0, so don't write anything in the hundreds. Finished!

*Or you could work out how much has to be added on to 169 to make 255 using a number line and the SSFF rule: **S**tart at the **S**econd number and **F**inish at the **F**irst number.*

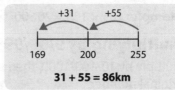

31 + 55 = 86km

1 In a traffic survey over three days, Samantha observed 180 vehicles in total. She recorded 45 cars on the first day and 40 on the second day. She also saw 61 other vehicles altogether. How many cars did she see on the third day?

2 Callum's mobile phone came with 200 free texts. He has replied to 67 texts sent by friends and has sent 49 of his own. How many of his free texts are left?

When you first learn about multiplication, you understand it as repeated addition, so 3 × 7 means 'three times 7', which is 7 + 7 + 7. You learn about division as 'sharing', but eventually you learn that it is also the opposite or 'inverse' of multiplication.

To use any of the methods of multiplication or division that you learn, you need to know the **number bonds** for multiplication – in other words, multiplication tables. From these you can learn how to multiply and divide numbers of any size.

Understanding multiplication and division

The following words or phrases are clues that a question may involve multiplication:

> **times   product   scale   each day, week, etc.   total**

…if you want to work out the 'total' number of maths lessons you have in a new term, you need to know how many maths lessons you have each week and multiply that number by the number of weeks in the term.

These words or phrases are clues that a question may involve division:

> **share   how many times/each   on average**
> **mean   fraction   remainder   left over**

…if there are six of you and you each want a 'share' of a packet of biscuits, you will have to divide the biscuits into six piles of biscuits.

Remember, sometimes when you do divisions there may be an amount left over – the **remainder**.

Multiplication and division skills

Multiplying by 10/100/1000

Move the digits in the number one, two or three places to the left. Fill empty places with zeros.

Example: $205 \times 100 = 20\,500$

Multiplying by 9/99/999

Multiply by 10/100/1000, then subtract the original number.

Example: $53 \times 9 = 530 - 53 = 477$

Repeated doubling

To multiply by 4, double twice, or to multiply by 8, double 3 times.

Example: 47×8: $47 \rightarrow 94 \rightarrow 188 \rightarrow 376$

Column and grid multiplication

236×34 could be done like this:

```
        2  3  6
  ×        3  4
        9₁ 4₂ 4    (236 × 4)
     7₁ 0₁ 8  0    (236 × 30)
     8  0  2  4
     1  1
```

Grid method:

×	200	30	6
30	6000	900	180
4	800	120	24

$6800 + 1020 + 204 = \mathbf{8024}$

Division by 10/100/1000

Move the digits in the number one, two or three places to the right, crossing the decimal point if you have to.

Example: $8650 \div 100 = 86.5$

Short division

$3654 \div 7$ could be done like this:

$$7 \overline{\smash{)}3\ 6\ {}^{1}5\ {}^{1}4} = 5\ 2\ 2$$

Other shortcuts

To divide by 5, double, then divide by 10.

Example: $775 \div 5$: $775 \rightarrow 1550 \rightarrow 155$

To divide by 4, halve, then halve again.

Example: $776 \div 4$: $776 \rightarrow 388 \rightarrow 194$

To divide large numbers by 11, 12, 13, 14… multiply by 10, 20, etc. first, then find the difference.

Example: $168 \div 14$: $14 \times 10 = 140 \rightarrow 168 - 140 = 28$
$28 = 2 \times 14$ so $(10 + 2) \times 14 = 168$ $168 \div 14 = 12$

Powers

Powers (**indices**) are used where there is repeated multiplication.
2^5 means $2 \times 2 \times 2 \times 2 \times 2$, but 5^2 means 5×5

Square roots

Finding a **square root** is the **inverse** of squaring. So because $3^2 = 9$, the square root of 9 is 3. This is written $\sqrt{9} = 3$.
Only **square numbers** have square roots that are whole numbers. For example, $\sqrt{10}$ is about 3.162

TRY IT OUT

Big breakfast

Choose a packet of your favourite cereal and work out how many packets you would need to buy if you ate a bowl of cereal every day for a month.

Take a look at the outside of the cereal packet. Look at the Recommended Daily Allowance (RDA) for different food types. See if you can calculate how many servings you would need to get your RDA.

Solving problems with multiplication and division

1 This question requires both multiplication and division.

 • Rashid sold 135 cups of juice at his school's summer fair. He charged 45p per cup. How much money did he take in total, in £ and pence?

   'Total' is a hint that you need to multiply.

   Use whatever method you prefer to calculate $135 \times 45 = 6075$

   This amount is in pence, so divide by 100 to convert to pounds: $6075 \div 100 = £60.75$

2 How do you know that this question involves division?

 • Eggs are packed in boxes of 6. How many boxes are needed to pack 3000 eggs?

   The number of boxes will be smaller than the number of eggs.

   You know that $30 \div 6 = 5$; this means that $300 \div 6 = 50$ and so $3000 \div 6 = 500$

TEST YOURSELF

1 Sophie didn't eat chocolate for 308 days. How many weeks was this?

2 A tray of Baxwells' soup holds 12 cans. Jez stacks 252 trays on to the shelves in the supermarket. How many cans are there altogether?

3 What is 5^4?
   What is the square root of 5^4?

Multiplying and dividing whole numbers

Solving problems involving the four operations

All four operations can be used together in a calculation. This can happen when you are solving a problem with a number of stages, or when a question is designed to test your understanding of how the operations work together.

Solving problems with several operations involves choosing an **operation** to suit each stage of the calculation. To work out the answer to a complicated calculation, you need to understand the natural order of the operations and how brackets can affect the order.

Understanding the order of operations

When different operations are mixed up, the parts of the calculation should be carried out in a certain order.

Multiplications and divisions should be done before additions and subtractions. So:

$5 + 2 \times 3 = 5 + 6 = 11$ *not* $5 + 2 \times 3 = 7 \times 3 = 21$

To get the answer 21, you would have to interfere with the natural order by using brackets. The bracket is calculated first:

$(5 + 2) \times 3$ $= 7 \times 3$ $= 21$

If operations at the same 'level' are mixed up, you do them in the order you find them.

$10 - 7 - 3 + 5$ $= 3 - 3 + 5$ $= 0 + 5$ $= 5$

However, brackets can alter the result here, too:

$10 - (7 - 3) + 5$ $= 10 - 4 + 5$ $= 6 + 5$ $= 11$

Remember the **BIDMAS** rule: **B**rackets first, then **I**ndices (powers), then **D**ivision and **M**ultiplication, then **A**ddition and **S**ubtraction.

Mixed operation skills

Multi-part problems

When you are solving a complex problem you need to plan the order of your calculations carefully. For example, you may need to do several multiplications, then add up the results of these multiplications.

Finding the **mean** of a set of numbers involves adding up the numbers to find the total, then dividing by the number of numbers.

Matching calculations

You may be given a calculation with the answer worked out, then asked to choose from a list of calculations that use the same or similar numbers. You might be looking for the calculation with the same answer as the example, or the one that's different.

Inserting brackets

You may have a calculation which, as it has been written in the question, doesn't give the answer shown. You have to put brackets in the right places to get the correct answer.

Solving problems with mixed operations

1 This problem uses a mixture of multiplication and addition.

- A shop sells collecting cards in different-sized packs.
  One Saturday, they sold 43 two-packs, 66 four-packs and 15 twelve-packs.
  How many cards did they sell altogether?

  *You need to work out the total number of cards for each type of pack,
  then add these totals together.*

  43 × 2 = 86, 66 × 4 = 264 and 15 × 12 = 180   *86 + 264 + 180 = 530*

2 In this question, slight changes are made to this calculation: (31 + 55) × 20 = 1720

  You have to find out how the changes affect the result of the calculation.

- Which of the following is correct?

  (31 + 55) × 21 = 1806

  The bracket totals 86, so multiplying by 1 more will add 86 to the result. This one is correct.

  1720 ÷ 20 = 31 + 55

  They have divided both sides of the original calculation by 20, so this is a true statement.

  (31 + 65) × 20 = 1920

  *The second number in the bracket has increased by 10.
  When this is multiplied by 20, 200 will be added to the answer, so this is right.*

  31 + 55 × 20 = 1720

  *The brackets have been removed, which means that 55 × 20 has to be done first, giving 1100.
  Adding this to 31 gives 1131 – wrong!*

  1720 ÷ 20 – 31 = 55

  *Although you have found the answer above, it's still worth checking this one,
  in case you have made a mistake. This is the same as the second one,
  with 31 taken away from both sides, so it is correct.*

TEST YOURSELF

1 Add brackets to this calculation to make it correct:

   76 – 48 ÷ 12 ÷ 3 = 7

2 In a computer game, you have to collect coins. Silver
   (S) coins are worth 20 points and gold (G) coins are
   worth 50 points. Jared and Callum play five levels.
   The table shows what they collected.

Level	1	2	3	4	5
Jared	8S, 3G	5S, 2G	5S, 0G	3S, 3G	7S, 4G
Callum	10S, 2G	4S, 4G	5S, 1G	2S, 2G	5S, 4G

   What is the difference between their mean scores?

   A no difference   **B** 1 point per level

   C 2 points per level   **D** 3 points per level

   E 5 points per level

TRY IT OUT

Four fours

This is a classic puzzle –
using four 4s, the four
operations and brackets,
how many different
numbers can you
make? Try to make all
the numbers between
1 and 20.

Examples:
3 = (4 + 4 + 4) ÷ 4
15 = 4 × 4 – 4 ÷ 4

Solving problems involving the four operations

Algebra

Algebra is a very powerful tool which allows you to use letters to represent numbers. Sometimes you do this because the value of a number is unknown; sometimes you do it because you can write down a rule connecting different numbers.

When you are trying to find an unknown number, you are solving an **equation**. A **rule** connecting numbers is called a **formula**. Sometimes you may be given a problem in words that can be solved easily using **algebra**.

Understanding algebraic notation

In algebra, addition and subtraction work the same way with letters as they do with numbers.

To add a and b together, write $a + b$; to subtract, write $a - b$.

Multiplication signs are not used. To show multiplication, numbers and letters are simply written next to one another.

So $2x$ means 'two times the number x', ab means 'multiply a by b', etc.

Division signs are used occasionally, but it is more usual to use the **fraction** style of division. So to divide the number P by 10, write $\frac{P}{10}$.

Expressions are made up of smaller pieces called **terms**. Here is an expression made from three terms: $c - 5d + 7$

Algebra skills

Substitution

Substitution is simply replacing letters by their number values. You need to be careful when dealing with multiplication – remember to put a times (×) sign in. So If you are told that $x = 12$, then $3x$ is not 312, but 3×12!

Using formulae

Using **formulae** usually just involves some substitution. For example, suppose the number of rods used to make a pattern of squares is $r = 3s + 1$. If you are told that a pattern has five squares, you would calculate $r = 3 \times 5 + 1 = 16$

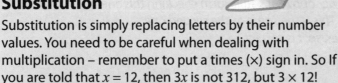

Solving equations

You can solve equations in two different ways:

- by **simplifying** the algebra a step at a time until you find the answer
- by using number machines.

Look at the rods and squares example again. You know that there is a pattern that uses 34 rods. How many squares does it have? You can use either of the following methods.

TRY IT OUT

Using formulae

Look for interactive Maths online games linked to algebra. Don't try to use any that have symbols you don't understand. You could start by entering 'Maths Zone' into a search engine – this should give you a list of Maths sites with interactive games.

Simplifying the algebra

$r = 3s + 1$

$34 = 3s + 1$ substitute value of r

$33 = 3s$ subtract 1 from both sides

$11 = s$ divide both sides by 3

Using number machines

squares $\rightarrow \boxed{\times 3} \rightarrow \boxed{+1} \rightarrow$ rods

Reversing the order and using **inverse** operations

squares $\leftarrow \boxed{\div 3} \leftarrow \boxed{-1} \leftarrow$ rods

So to find the number of squares:

$34 - 1 = 33; 33 \div 3 = 11$

Simplifying

Simplifying involves collecting the same types of **like terms** together in an expression. In the expression $3u + 2v - u + 7v$, you can reorder the terms:

$3u - u + 2v + 7v$

Then the two terms with u in them and the two terms with v can be combined:

$2u + 9v$

Solving problems with algebra

1 This problem contains a more complex equation.

- If $8n - 5 = 5n + 7$, what does n equal?

  This equation needs to be simplified. Whatever you do to one side of an equation, you must do the same to the other side. The easiest way to simplify this equation is to first get rid of the -5 on the left-hand side. You might think that subtracting 7 on both sides would be a good place to start, but this would leave -12 on the left-hand side and make the equation more complex to solve: $8n - 12 = 5n$. So:

  Add 5 to both sides to get rid of the -5: $8n = 5n + 12$

  Then subtract 5n from both sides: $3n = 12$

  Then divide both sides by 3 to find the value of n: $n = 4$

2 This question tests whether you can match the algebra to a situation.

- On a train there are x standard class carriages with 84 seats each and y first class carriages with 60 seats each. How many seats are available on the train altogether? Choose the right answer.

  A $144xy$ **B** $84 + x + 60 + y$ **C** $84x + 60y$

  D $84y + 60x$ **E** $144 + x + y$

  You need to multiply the number of seats in a standard carriage by the number of carriages: 84 times x, written 84x. Do the same for the first class carriages: 60y. Now add these together: 84x + 60y, so C is the correct answer.

3 This question tests whether you can substitute values into a formula.

- If $p = 2$, $q = 5$, $r = -1$ and $Y = 3p + qr$, what is the value of Y?

  Write out the formula: $Y = 3p + qr$

  Substitute the numbers: $Y = 3 \times 2 + 5 \times -1$

  Do the calculation: $Y = 6 + -5$, so $Y = 1$

TEST YOURSELF

1 What is the value of x, if $6x + 4 = 2x + 10$?

2 Two years ago, Joyti's brother was y years old. How old will he be in five years' time?

   A $y + 7$ **B** $y - 7$ **C** $y + 5$

   D $y + 3$ **E** $y - 2$

Fractions, decimals and percentages are all different ways of representing parts of a whole. Fractions are numbers that 'fill in the gaps' between the whole numbers.

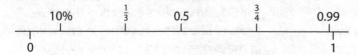

Every fraction can be written as a decimal or as a percentage. So, for example, $\frac{1}{2}$ = 0.5 or 50%. As fractions are just numbers, you can calculate with them just as you can with whole numbers.

What to expect

In the test, some questions may ask you to find a fraction of an amount. Sometimes these questions have a context, sometimes they are pure calculations. You may be asked to compare fractions or find equivalents – this is also true of questions involving ratio.

Some questions in the test papers will be multiple-choice. To answer them, you need to select the correct answer from the choices given. For example, you may be asked to identify the largest number from a list of fractions, decimals and percentages.

Fraction, decimal and percentage skills

1   Fractions and ratios are quite similar in that the same thing can be written in several different ways.

$\frac{1}{2}, \frac{2}{4}, \frac{3}{6}, \frac{5}{10}$ and $\frac{25}{50}$ are all examples of the same fraction.

4 : 3, 8 : 6, 20 : 15, 100 : 75 are all examples of the same ratio.

In both cases, the version containing the smallest whole numbers is in the simplest form, or lowest terms.

2   You can use all of your skills in calculating with whole numbers when you are using decimals.

23 + 125 = 148

This means that 2.3 + 12.5 = 14.8, 0.23 + 1.25 = 1.48, 0.023 + 0.125 = 0.148, etc.

The decimal calculations are related to the whole number ones by factors of 10, 100, etc.

3   Money calculations rely on decimals. There are also shortcuts that can speed up your work.

5 magazines at £2.99 each cost a total of £14.95

£2.99 is one penny less than £3.

5 × £3 = £15

Now subtract 5p to get £14.95

Introducing fractions, decimals and percentages

4 Questions about the equivalence of percentages and fractions are sometimes presented using diagrams.

25% of this grid is coloured pink.

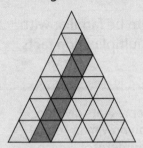

The whole grid contains 36 triangles.

9 of these are coloured pink.

So the fraction coloured pink is $\frac{9}{36} = \frac{1}{4}$

$\frac{1}{4} = 25\%$

TIPS FOR SUCCESS

Equivalents

- It's very important to know the equivalent decimals and percentages for fractions. The more of these you can remember, the less time you will spend having to work them out. It's a bit like knowing the multiplication tables well.

  What are the decimals for $\frac{1}{4}$, $\frac{1}{2}$ and $\frac{3}{4}$?

  What fractions are represented by 10%, 20%, 30% and so on?

What you will learn

In this section you will learn about these topics:

- fractions and equivalent fractions
- fraction calculations
- decimals
- equivalence of fractions, decimals and percentages
- percentage calculations
- ratio and proportion.

In the test, you can expect to find questions like these.

- Here is a list of fractions, decimals and percentages.

  $\frac{1}{4}$ 20% $\frac{6}{25}$ 0.26 $\frac{13}{50}$

  Which *two* are the smallest?

  A $\frac{1}{4}$ and 20%

  B 0.26 and $\frac{13}{50}$

  C 20% and $\frac{6}{25}$

  D $\frac{6}{25}$ and 0.26

  E $\frac{1}{4}$ and $\frac{6}{25}$

  Change them all to decimals:

  $\frac{1}{4} = 0.25$ 20% = 0.2 $\frac{6}{25} = 0.24$ 0.26 $\frac{13}{50} = 0.26$

  0.2 and 0.24 are the smallest, so the correct answer is C.

- Linden School raised some money for charity on their Fun Day.

  They divided the money between Childline and Save the Children in the ratio 2 : 3. £180 went to Childline.

  How much did they raise altogether?

  The ratio 2 : 3 means that the money was divided into 2 + 3 = 5 shares.

  2 of the shares = £180 so one share was £90.

  The total amount was 5 × £90 = £450

Fractions

Fractions represent parts of a whole, but they are also numbers in their own right. You could find a position on a number line for any fraction, and any arithmetic you can do with whole numbers, you can do with fractions.

To work quickly and accurately with **fractions**, you need to be familiar with **factors** and **multiples** (see page 22), which depend on multiplication facts.

Understanding fractions

Fractions have two parts separated by a **horizontal** line that represents division. The number below the line is the **denominator**, which tells you how many equal parts a whole is divided into. The number above is called the **numerator**, which tells you how many of these equal parts make up the fraction.

Fractions with a numerator of 1 are called **unit fractions**.

Examples: $\frac{1}{2}$, $\frac{1}{4}$, $\frac{1}{10}$

Two fractions that are made up of different numbers may represent the same part of a whole. These are called **equivalent fractions**.

Examples: $\frac{1}{2} = \frac{2}{4}$ and $\frac{3}{4} = \frac{9}{12}$

For every set of equivalent fractions, there is one that contains the smallest possible whole numbers. That fraction is said to be in **lowest terms** or **simplest form**.

A **mixed number** or mixed fraction has a whole number part and a fraction part. An **improper fraction** has a numerator that is bigger than its denominator, and is **equivalent** to a mixed number.

Example: $1\frac{1}{2}$ is read as 'one and a half' and is equivalent to $\frac{3}{2}$ ($1 = \frac{2}{2}$ so $\frac{2}{2} + \frac{1}{2} = \frac{3}{2}$)

Fraction skills

Equivalent fractions and lowest terms

Given any fraction, it is easy to create an equivalent fraction for it. Simply multiply its numerator and denominator by the same number, or divide its numerator and denominator by the same number.

Example: $\frac{6}{10}$ If you multiply the numerator and denominator by 5, you get $\frac{30}{50}$.

If you divide the numerator and denominator by 2, you get $\frac{3}{5}$. $\frac{3}{5}$ is in lowest terms.

This diagram shows how the fractions are equivalent.

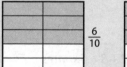 $\frac{6}{10}$  $\frac{30}{50}$ 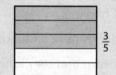 $\frac{3}{5}$

A fraction is in lowest terms if the **highest common factor** (HCF) of its numerator and denominator is 1.

Ordering fractions

To write a set of fractions in order, you need to find equivalent fractions with the same denominator, so you can compare numerators. This **common denominator** will be a **common multiple** of the denominators of the fractions, and if you can find the **lowest (or least) common denominator** or **lowest (or least) common multiple**, this will keep the numbers as small as possible.

Example: Which is bigger, $\frac{5}{9}$ or $\frac{7}{12}$?

The LCM (lowest common multiple) of 9 and 12 is 36, so convert both fractions to 36ths.

$\frac{5}{9} = \frac{20}{36}$ (the numerator 5 and denominator 9 are multiplied by 4 to convert to 36ths).

$\frac{7}{12} = \frac{21}{36}$ (the numerator 7 and denominator 12 are multiplied by 3 to convert to 36ths).

So $\frac{7}{12}$ is bigger.

Adding and subtracting fractions

Use the same technique of matching denominators to add and subtract fractions.

Example: $\frac{3}{4} + \frac{1}{2} \quad = \frac{3}{4} + \frac{2}{4} \quad = \frac{5}{4} \quad = 1\frac{1}{4}$

Solving problems with fractions

1 This question involves subtracting and comparing fractions using a common denominator.

- Which of these fractions is closest to $\frac{1}{2}$? $\quad \frac{1}{3}, \frac{3}{4}, \frac{5}{6}, \frac{2}{3}, \frac{5}{12}$

You need a common denominator for 2, 3, 4, 6 and 12. 12 is the LCM, so write all the fractions as 12ths.

fraction	$\frac{1}{3}$	$\frac{3}{4}$	$\frac{5}{6}$	$\frac{2}{3}$	$\frac{5}{12}$
convert to 12ths	$\frac{4}{12}$	$\frac{9}{12}$	$\frac{10}{12}$	$\frac{8}{12}$	$\frac{5}{12}$
difference from $\frac{1}{2}$	$\frac{6}{12} - \frac{4}{12} = \frac{2}{12}$	$\frac{9}{12} - \frac{6}{12} = \frac{3}{12}$	$\frac{10}{12} - \frac{6}{12} = \frac{4}{12}$	$\frac{8}{12} - \frac{6}{12} = \frac{2}{12}$	$\frac{6}{12} - \frac{5}{12} = \frac{1}{12}$

So $\frac{5}{12}$ is the closest.

2 This question tests your knowledge of mixed numbers and **simplifying** fractions.

- Write $\frac{63}{27}$ as a mixed number in lowest terms.

There are two jobs to do: simplify the fraction and write it as a mixed number.
The numerator and denominator are both multiples of 9, so divide top and bottom by 9 to get $\frac{7}{3}$. Now write as a mixed number:

$7 = 2 \times 3 + 1$, so $\frac{7}{3} = 2\frac{1}{3}$

TRY IT OUT

Washing number line

If you have a washing line, try putting a clothes peg exactly $\frac{1}{2}, \frac{1}{3}, \frac{1}{4}, \frac{1}{6}$, etc. of the way along it. Which fractions are easy to see and which are harder?

TEST YOURSELF

1 Write these fractions in order of size from smallest to largest:

A $\frac{11}{20}$ **B** $\frac{4}{5}$ **C** $\frac{1}{2}$

D $\frac{3}{4}$ **E** $\frac{7}{10}$

2 Which pair of these fractions add up to 1 whole?

A $\frac{5}{8}$ **B** $\frac{2}{8}$ **C** $\frac{1}{2}$

D $\frac{3}{4}$ **E** $\frac{7}{8}$

3 Write $4\frac{3}{8}$ as an improper fraction.

Fraction calculations

Calculating with fractions usually involves finding a fraction of an amount. You may need to compare the results of these calculations to answer a question.

To work with **fraction** calculations, you need to understand how fraction notation works (see page 36). Make sure you know what the **numerator** and **denominator** of a fraction mean and that you can find **equivalent fractions**.

Understanding fraction calculations

A **unit fraction** of an amount just involves division. So to find $\frac{1}{2}$, you divide by 2, to find $\frac{1}{5}$, you divide by 5, etc.

…so if you were going to get a $\frac{1}{5}$ share of 20 sweets, you would divide 20 by 5 to work out what your share was.

To find other fractions, find the unit fraction and then multiply by the numerator. So to find $\frac{2}{5}$, you divide by 5 and multiply by 2.

…so if your share increased to $\frac{2}{5}$ you would multiply the $\frac{1}{5}$ share by 2.

Fraction calculation skills

Speed

Numerator is one less than denominator is a *trick* that can help you with the speed of your calculations. For example, suppose you want to work out $\frac{3}{4}$ of £96.

The standard method would involve finding $\frac{1}{4}$ (£96 ÷ 4 = £24), then multiplying by 3 (£24 × 3 = £72).

However, because the numerator is one less than the denominator, this amount is just $\frac{1}{4}$ *less* than the whole amount. So you could subtract £24 from £96 to get the answer. This works just as well with other kinds of fraction: to find $\frac{7}{8}$, subtract $\frac{1}{8}$ from the whole, to find $\frac{9}{10}$, subtract $\frac{1}{10}$, etc.

Working backwards

Working backwards is helpful if you are told what a fraction of an amount is, and asked to work out the whole amount.

For example, if 240 grams of sugar is used to make a cake and this is $\frac{3}{8}$ of the weight of the cake, what does the whole cake weigh? To answer this you have to find $\frac{1}{8}$ first, so divide by 3:

240 ÷ 3 = 80g

Now you know $\frac{1}{8}$ of the weight, multiply by 8 to get the whole weight:

80 × 8 = 640g

Finding the fraction

Sometimes you need to know what fraction one amount is of another amount. For example, the weight of the fruit in the cake mentioned above is 200 grams. What fraction of the weight of the cake is this? To answer the question, just write the fraction $\frac{\text{weight of sugar}}{\text{weight of whole cake}}$, then cancel to **lowest terms**:

$\frac{200}{640} = \frac{20}{64} = \frac{10}{32} = \frac{5}{16}$ Finished!

Solving problems with fraction calculations

1 This is a straightforward fraction calculation, but you need to read the question very carefully. The word 'not' is very important!

- 360 people go to see a film. $\frac{3}{5}$ of them have popcorn. How many people did *not* have popcorn?

   First divide by 5 to find $\frac{1}{5}$ of the number of people:

   $360 \div 5 = 72$

   Now you have a choice of two methods. You could either:

   multiply by 3 to find $\frac{3}{5}$

   $72 \times 3 = 216$ *people*

   then subtract this from 360 to get 144 people; or you find $\frac{2}{5}$, the fraction who didn't have popcorn:

   multiply $\frac{1}{5}$ by 2 to find $\frac{2}{5}$

   $72 \times 2 = 144$

2 This question involves finding one fraction from another.

- Asif bought a pack of collecting cards. $\frac{5}{8}$ of the pack were cards he wanted to keep, and he gave me the 18 cards that were left over. How many cards did he keep?

   If Asif kept $\frac{5}{8}$ of the cards, he must have given me $\frac{3}{8}$.

   So divide by 3 to find $\frac{1}{8}$ $\qquad$ $18 \div 3 = 6$

   Now multiply by 5 to find $\frac{5}{8}$ $\qquad$ $6 \times 5 = 30$ cards

3 In this question you express a number as a fraction of a total – you need to be able to do this when you are answering questions on **probability**.

- The table shows the results of a survey into how pupils in class 6M travel to school.

transport	walking	cycling	by car	by bus
pupils	5	5	8	12

   What fraction of the class come to school by bus?

   First you need to know how many pupils there are in the class:

   $5 + 5 + 8 + 12 = 30$

   Now work out the fraction: $\frac{12}{30} = \frac{6}{15} = \frac{2}{5}$

TRY IT OUT

Fractions everywhere

You can find fractions everywhere. Try these and any others you can think of:

Hopefully, if you're taking 11+ soon, you're reading a book! What fraction of it have you read? Use your current page number and the total number of pages in the book to find out.

What fraction of this year has gone by? Work out how many days have elapsed since the start of the year to help you (and is it a leap year?).

TEST YOURSELF

1 What fraction of the numbers in this list are **prime**?

   1 3 5 7 9 11 13 15 17

2 Sunita spent £56 on some new trainers. After this she had $\frac{3}{10}$ of her money left. How much money does she have left?

3 Eric eats $\frac{2}{3}$ of a bag of sweets. Joanna eats $\frac{2}{3}$ of what is left, then Zoltan eats $\frac{2}{3}$ of what Joanna left. There are now 2 sweets in the bag. How many were there to start with?

Decimals should really be called 'decimal fractions', but we use them so much that the name has just been shortened to 'decimals'.

Decimals extend our tens-based number system, so we can use it to describe parts of a whole using the same idea of place value that we have for whole numbers. It also means that all the calculation methods you know for whole numbers will work with decimals.

Understanding decimals

A decimal point is used to separate the whole number part of a decimal from the fractional part. The places to the right of the decimal point represent tenths, hundredths, thousandths, etc. If a number is between 0 and 1, you usually write a 0 in the units place to avoid confusion. The decimal numbers in this table are ordered from largest (top) to smallest (bottom).

…our money uses a decimal system, so if you had £7.35 in your wallet, this is 7 whole pounds, 3 tenths of a pound and 5 hundredths.

Multiplying or dividing a decimal by ten moves its digits one place, multiplying or dividing by 100 moves its digits two places, etc.

units		tenths	hundredths	thousandths	
1	.	5			one whole and five tenths
0	.	2	4		two tenths and four hundredths
0	.	0	1		one hundredth
0	.	0	0	5	five thousandths

Example: $35.25 \times 10 = 352.5$; $35.25 \div 10 = 3.525$

$35.25 \times 100 = 3525$; $35.25 \div 100 = 0.3525$

…if you had £7.35 in your wallet, this is $7.35 \times 100 = 735$ pence.

Decimal skills

Putting decimals in order of size is a good way to build familiarity with how they work and increase your confidence when answering questions about decimals.

Adding and subtracting decimals

When you are adding and subtracting decimals, use the same methods as for whole numbers.

This shows the column addition of 2.55 and 4.7

Note how 4.7 has been written as 4.70 so that both numbers have the same number of decimal places.

```
  2 . 5 5
+ 4 . 7 0
---------
  7 . 2 5
    ₁
```

Multiplying and dividing decimals

When you are multiplying and dividing decimals, it is often simpler to work with whole numbers, then adjust the answer so it is the right size. For example, suppose you had to multiply 5.2 by 0.6

First, work with the digits as if they were whole numbers:

$52 \times 6 = 312$

Now adjust each number until it's the right size:

$5.2 \times 6 = 31.2$ (ten times smaller) and $5.2 \times 0.6 = 3.12$ (ten times smaller again).

When dividing, be very careful when adjusting the answer. For example, to work out $12.6 \div 0.02$, start with $126 \div 2 = 63$. So $12.6 \div 2 = 6.3$, but $12.6 \div 0.02 = 630$ (dividing by a number that is 100 times smaller makes the answer 100 times bigger).

In the test you may be asked to find something like '0.6 of 5.2'. In this question 'of' just means 'multiplied by'.

Rounding decimals

Rounding with decimals is just like rounding with whole numbers. Rounding 'to one decimal place' means rounding to the nearest tenth, 'to two decimal places' to the nearest hundredth, etc. The '5 and over' rounding up rule applies here too.

Example: Here is the number 4.1635 rounded in different ways.

Rounding	Result	Comments
nearest whole number	4	closer to 4 than 5
1 decimal place (1 d.p.)	4.2	closer to 4.2 than 4.1
2 decimal places (2 d.p.)	4.16	closer to 4.16 than 4.17
3 decimal places (3 d.p.)	4.164	halfway between 4.163 and 4.164 so round up

Solving problems with decimals

1 In this problem you have to compare the results of two decimal calculations.

- Which is bigger, 2.4×0.4 or $0.285 \div 0.3$?

   First do the multiplication:
   $24 \times 4 = 96$, so $2.4 \times 4 = 9.6$, so $2.4 \times 0.4 = 0.96$

   Now the division:
   $285 \div 3 = 95$, so $28.5 \div 3 = 9.5$, $2.85 \div 3 = 0.95$ and $0.285 \div 3 = 0.095$, finally, $0.285 \div 0.3 = 0.95$ So 2.4×0.4 is bigger.

2 Here you have to find the 'odd one out' among numbers that round to a particular answer.

- Which of these numbers, rounded to 1 decimal place, does *not* round to 3.1?
   3.08   3.054   3.15   3.145   3.05

   Check all the numbers.
   $3.08 \to 3.1$ $3.054 \to 3.1$ $3.15 \to 3.2$ $3.145 \to 3.1$ $3.05 \to 3.1$
   So 3.15 is the 'odd one out' because it does not round to 3.1

TRY IT OUT

Multipacks

Find out how much some of the multipack grocery items cost that your family buys. Divide these amounts by the number of items in the pack to find the cost of 1 item. The answers can be surprising!

Ideas: water bottles and soft drinks, cans of beans or tins of fish, toilet rolls, tea bags, sweets.

TEST YOURSELF

1 16.285714

   Jasmine got this answer to a money question in pounds on her calculator. What is her answer correct to the nearest penny?

2 Mr Pickett spent £25.50 buying 30 guppies for his aquarium. How much did each fish cost? Circle the letter beside the correct answer.

   A £1.20   **B** 85p   **C** 95p   **D** 75p   **E** £1.05

3 What number does the arrow point to on this number line?

Finding equivalents

Decimals and percentages are different ways of writing fractions. Every fraction can be written as a decimal or a percentage.

A **percentage** is simply a short way of writing a **fraction** with **denominator** 100. So 1% means $\frac{1}{100}$, 5% means $\frac{5}{100}$, 20% means $\frac{20}{100}$, etc.

Understanding equivalents

The connection between percentages and **decimals** is very simple.

For example, $1\% = \frac{1}{100} = 0.01$ and $10\% = \frac{10}{100} = \frac{1}{10} = 0.1$

So for most simple percentages, you can immediately see the decimal **equivalent**.

For example, 24% is 0.24

Finding a fraction that is equivalent to a decimal is also straightforward.

Taking the last example, 0.24 is $\frac{2}{10} + \frac{4}{100}$, which is the same as $\frac{24}{100}$.

You can then cancel this to **lowest terms**:
both the **numerator** and denominator are **multiples** of 4, so $\frac{24}{100} = \frac{6}{25}$.

There are a number of equivalents that you should try to memorise:

fraction	decimal	percentage		fraction	decimal	percentage
$\frac{1}{2}$	0.5	50%		$\frac{3}{5}$	0.6	60%
$\frac{1}{4}$	0.25	25%		$\frac{1}{4}$	0.8	80%
$\frac{3}{4}$	0.75	75%		$\frac{1}{20}$	0.05	5%
$\frac{1}{10}$	0.1	10%		$\frac{1}{25}$	0.04	4%
$\frac{1}{5}$	0.2	20%		$\frac{1}{50}$	0.02	2%
$\frac{2}{5}$	0.4	40%		$\frac{1}{100}$	0.01	1%

…so if you look at a bill that includes VAT at 20%, you should see that the VAT is one-fifth of the total amount.

Equivalence skills

Recurring decimals

Some fractions have decimals that repeat or *recur*. These are some common ones you should recognise:

$\frac{1}{3} = 0.3333\ldots$ $\frac{2}{3} = 0.6666\ldots$

Fractional and decimal percentages

Percentages do not have to contain only whole numbers. For example:

$0.125 = 12\frac{1}{2}\% = \frac{12.5}{100} = \frac{25}{200} = \frac{1}{8}$ $\frac{1}{3} = 33\frac{1}{3}\%$

Ordering

You may be asked to take a set of fractions, decimals and percentages and place them in order of size. To compare them, it may be easiest to work in decimals.

Targets

Some questions ask you to find the number in a list that is closest to a special number, perhaps 1 or 0.5. The procedure is similar to that for ordering, as it involves comparing values.

Solving problems with equivalence

1 This question asks you to find an 'odd one out'.

- Four of these have the same value.
  Which one is different?

$\frac{1}{20}$ 5% $\frac{5}{100}$ 0.05   0.20

First notice that 5% and $\frac{5}{100}$ are the same,

so you are looking for the number which is different from these.

$\frac{1}{20} = \frac{5}{100}$, $0.05 = \frac{5}{100}$ but $0.20 = \frac{20}{100}$,

so this is the odd one out.

2 This is an ordering question.

- Which of these is the largest?

$\frac{3}{4}$ 71% $\frac{37}{50}$ $72\frac{1}{2}$%   0.7

Change them all to decimals.

original	$\frac{3}{4}$	71%	$\frac{37}{50}$	$72\frac{1}{2}$%	0.7
decimal	0.75	0.71	0.74	0.725	0.7

So $\frac{3}{4}$ is the biggest.

3 This is a 'target' question.

- Which of these is the closest to $\frac{1}{2}$?

45%   0.4 $\frac{13}{25}$ 53% $\frac{11}{20}$

Change them to decimals.

original	45%	0.4	$\frac{13}{25}$	53%	$\frac{11}{20}$
decimal	0.45	0.4	0.52	0.53	0.55
difference from 0.5	0.05	0.1	0.02	0.03	0.05

So $\frac{13}{25}$ is the closest.

TEST YOURSELF

1 Find the smallest of these quantities.

A 1.8%   **B** 0.18   **C** $\frac{1}{18}$

D 0.081   **E** 0.108

2 Which of these is closest to 1?

A 0.99   **B** 95%   **C** 1.05

D 103%   **E** $\frac{49}{50}$

3 Which of these does not have the same value as the others?

A $\frac{1}{5}$ **B** 0.2   **C** 2%

D $\frac{2}{10}$ **E** $\frac{5}{25}$

4 What percentage of this grid is shaded?

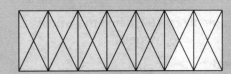

Calculating with percentages is very similar to calculating with fractions – because it's actually the same thing!

Finding a **percentage** of something usually hinges on finding 1% first – in other words, dividing by 100. You can then multiply by the number of percent to obtain your answer.

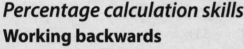

Understanding percentage calculations

The 'standard' method for calculating a percentage is to divide by 100 and then multiply by the number of percent. However, as you have seen (page 42), percentages have **equivalent fractions**, and it may often be easier to use these than work through the 'divide by 100 and multiply' method.

Examples: given an amount of £400, find:

10%	This is equal to $\frac{1}{10}$,	so £400 ÷ 10 = £40
25%	This is equal to $\frac{1}{4}$,	so £400 ÷ 4 = £100
40%	This is equal to 0.4,	so £400 × 0.4 = £160

You could also use $\frac{2}{5} \rightarrow \frac{1}{5}$ is £400 ÷ 5 = £80, so $\frac{2}{5}$ = £160

...*so if you put 40% of your pocket money away each week to save up for something, that's $\frac{2}{5}$.*

Percentage calculation skills

Working backwards

If you know the value of a percentage of an amount, you can find the amount by working backwards. Either find 1% and multiply by 100, or use an equivalent fraction.

Example: In a survey, 42 people said they preferred white bread to brown. This was 70% of the people who were asked. How many people were asked?

Method 1: to find 1%, divide by 70:
    42 ÷ 70 = 0.6 people.

Now multiply by 100 to find the whole:
    0.6 × 100 = 60 people.

Method 2: 70% = $\frac{7}{10}$,
    so divide by 7 to find $\frac{1}{10}$.
    42 ÷ 7 = 6 people.

Now multiply by 10 to find the whole:
    6 × 10 = 60 people, as before.

Using an equivalent fraction can often make the calculation much simpler.

Finding the percentage

Finding a percentage is rather like expressing one amount as a **fraction** of another.

Example: Out of 75 boxes of eggs, 18 contained at least one broken egg. What percentage of the boxes had a broken egg?

First write a fraction: $\frac{18}{75}$ of the boxes had a broken egg. If you can find an equivalent fraction with a denominator of 100, you have found the percentage:

$\frac{18}{75} = \frac{6}{25} = \frac{24}{100}$

So the percentage is 24%.

Percentage change

It may be that a percentage is added on to an amount (increase, interest or tax) or taken off an amount (decrease, discount or reduction). To work out the percentage change, simply calculate the percentage of the original amount and add it to or subtract it from the amount.

Solving problems with percentage calculations

1 In this question you have to compare several amounts.

● Which of these has the biggest value?

25% of £40 $\frac{1}{10}$ of £90 $\frac{1}{3}$ of £33   0.6 of £15   12% of £80

You need to calculate each part.

25% of £40 = $\frac{1}{4}$ of £40 = £10 $\frac{1}{10}$ of £90 = £90 ÷ 10 = £9

$\frac{1}{3}$ of £33 = £33 ÷ 3 = £11   0.6 of £15 = 0.6 × £15 = £9

12% of £80 = 0.12 × £80 = 1.2 × £8 = £9.60

So $\frac{1}{3}$ of £33 is the biggest.

2 In this question you have to find one percentage from another.

● A factory produces steel girders. On one day, 98% of the girders had no defects.
These are called 'good' girders. 100 had defects and were 'bad' girders.
How many good girders were there?

If 98% were good, that means that 2% were bad.
So 2% = 100 girders. Divide by 2 to find that 1% = 50 girders.

Now multiply by 100 to see that 100% = 5000 girders.

5000 – 100 = 4900 good girders.

3 Look for the clues in this problem to find the percentage.

● The results of a magazine survey showed that these were the
figures for how many hours people spent asleep at night.

4 or fewer	5–6	7–8	9–10	11 or more
1	42	25	10	2

What percentage of the people surveyed got 9 or more hours of sleep?

The number who took part in the survey is 1 + 42 + 25 + 10 + 2 = 80

The number of people sleeping 9 hours or more is 10 + 2 = 12

So the fraction is $\frac{12}{80} = \frac{3}{20} = \frac{15}{100}$

The answer is 15%.

TRY IT OUT

Recipes

Have a look at some recipes. See if you
can work out the percentage of the total
weight that each ingredient takes up.

For example, if all the ingredients for a
casserole weigh 1500 grams and you
need 225 grams of carrots, this is:

$\frac{225}{1500} = \frac{450}{3000} = \frac{45}{300} = \frac{15}{100} = 15\%$

TEST YOURSELF

1 St Mark's School sold 500 tickets for
a raffle. 4% of the tickets won a prize.
How many tickets did not win a prize?

2 Which answer is different from the
others?

A 50% of £50   **B** 25% of £100

C $\frac{5}{8}$ of £40   **D** 30% of £75

E 10% of £250

3 A jar of jam used to cost £1.20 but
the price has increased by 20%.
What does it cost now?

Ratio and proportion

Quantities that are in proportion to each other work in a very particular way – if one is multiplied by a number, the other is multiplied by the same number. A similar thing happens if you divide.

This means that things that are proportional to each other always stay in a fixed **ratio**. For example, when you measure a length in metres and then measure the same length in centimetres, the number of centimetres is always 100 times the number of metres, and if you double the number of metres, you have to double the number of centimetres.

Understanding ratio and proportion

Suppose you see a field of cows. You might not know how many cows there are, but you know that every cow has four legs. So they are in **proportion** to each other – there are four times as many legs as there are cows. The ratio legs : cows is 4 : 1. The number of legs is proportional to the number of cows because they are in a fixed ratio.

Ratio and proportion skills

Equivalent ratios

Ratios have a good deal in common with **fractions**. Ratios containing different numbers can be **equivalent** to each other. Suppose that a tank contains 30 orange fish and 20 yellow fish. Then the ratio is orange : yellow = 30 : 20. However, you could also say that in the tank, for every three orange fish, there are two yellow fish. So the ratio can also be written as 3 : 2. The ratio has been cancelled to '**lowest terms**', just like a fraction.

So to find **equivalent ratios**, simply multiply or divide the numbers in the ratio by the same thing.

Proportional division

You can also divide up amounts according to a ratio. This is called proportional division.

Suppose that Years 5 and 6 in a school have raised £180 for new equipment.

There are 30 pupils in Year 5 and 24 in Year 6. They decide to share the money in proportion to the number of people in the classes.

The ratio is Y5 : Y6 = 30 : 24 = 5 : 4 in lowest terms. So there are 5 + 4 = 9 'shares' available.

Each 'share' will be £180 ÷ 9 = £20. Year 5 will get 5 × £20 = £100 and Year 6 will get 4 × £20 = £80

Proportional reasoning

Proportional reasoning can be used for many different types of problem. For example, 5 miles is almost exactly 8 kilometres. How many miles is 40km?

The ratio miles : km = 5 : 8 = ? : 40. To turn 8 into 40 you multiply by 5, so do this to the number of miles as well. The missing number in the ratio must be 25.

So 40 kilometres = 25 miles.

Solving problems with ratio and proportion

1 The measurements on a map and those in reality are connected by ratios, usually with quite large numbers.

- A map of the UK is drawn to a scale of 1 : 200 000. Two towns are 15cm apart on the map. What is the real distance between them?

  1cm on the map represents 200 000cm in reality.

  200 000cm = 2000m = 2km.

  So 15cm represents 30km.
  The towns are 30km apart.

2 This question uses simple proportional reasoning.

- At a school play, the ratio of adults to children in the audience was 7 : 3. If there were 24 children in the audience, how many adults were there?

  The audience has been divided into 7 + 3 = 10 'shares'.

  3 shares = 24 people,

  so 1 share = 8 people.

  The number of adults was 7 × 8 = 56

3 In this question, you use the idea of 'one share' again.

- Jude's recipe for nut roast serves 4 people and needs 600 grams of nuts. She wants to cook a nut roast for 6 people. What weight of nuts does she need?

  4 people require 600g,

  so a nut roast for 1 person would require 600 ÷ 4 = 150g.

  Now multiply by 6 to get the new quantity: 6 ×150g = 900g.

TRY IT OUT

Old units

Do some research on the internet about old units of measurement such as 'rods' and 'furlongs'. These were often related to each other by unusual ratios – certainly not tens and hundreds!

TEST YOURSELF

1 Which of these ratios is not equivalent to 16 : 12?

   A 20 : 15   **B** 8 : 6   **C** 24 : 16

   D 36 : 27   **E** 32 : 24

2 In a choir, the ratio of boys to girls is 5 : 3. There are 18 girls in the choir. How many children are in the choir altogether?

3 Will has just finished building a model plane with a scale of 1 : 72. The model is 20cm long. How long is the real plane?

4 This **pie chart** shows the **percentages** of different kinds of jam sold in a supermarket in one week.

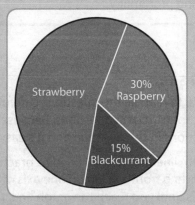

They sold 45 jars of blackcurrant jam. How many jars of strawberry jam did they sell?

Introducing charts and data

Drawing charts is one of the ways you can make a large amount of information easier to understand. These pieces of information are called data. The type of chart used will vary, depending on what features of the data you want to concentrate on.

Bar charts and pictograms are useful for comparing frequencies; pie charts clearly show what fraction of the whole each part takes up.

A line graph is used when a quantity varies with time, or where a relationship between two different quantities can be shown.

If the information is *qualitative* (descriptions or categories), charting is all that can really be done with it, though it is possible to identify the modal item – the one with the highest frequency. If the information is *quantitative* (numerical), you can process the data to calculate an average value – the median or mean.

Calculating probabilities is also closely linked to the collection of data. Sometimes analysing a situation mathematically allows you to calculate a probability; sometimes you need to look at the results of experiments to find an estimate.

What to expect

In the test, you will be expected to extract information from charts. This might involve reading a single value or combining several values. You may also have to compare values from one chart, or even between two different charts. You may have to answer questions about grids with two different line graphs on them.

Calculations with averages are usually straightforward, though you may be asked to 'work backwards', perhaps to find a value missing from your data.

Some questions in the test papers may be multiple-choice. To answer them, you need to select the correct answer from the choices given. For example, from a list of statements about a chart, you may be asked to find the one that is incorrect. The same type of question is often asked about a situation involving probability.

Data skills

It is vital to read all the questions carefully before you do them! This is especially important with data questions, because you need to interpret the data as well as the instructions in the question and it's easy to miss something.

1 With line graphs, you need to practise the skill of 'reading across'. This involves starting from a value on one axis of the graph, following a line at right angles to this until you reach the graph line, then turning through 90° and following a line across to the other axis, where you can read off the required value. You can always draw lines on the grid to help you if you wish.

Write your answers on the lines provided. When you are given a choice of answers, you will need to circle the letter (A, B, C, D or E) you think is correct. Some questions ask you to mark a diagram. Please use an extra sheet of paper for your workings. *Do not write answers in the 'Mark' column.*

You may not use a calculator.

Mark

Numbers and their properties

1 Round the number 3746 to the nearest hundred.

_____

2 In the number 2615 the value of the digit 6 is six hundred. What is the value of the digit 5? Circle the correct letter.

  A Five hundred   **B** Five units   **C** Five tens   **D** Five thousand   **E** Five tenths

3 Fill in the two missing numbers in this number series.

  30   33   _____   39   _____   45

4 Circle two prime numbers in this list.

  1   4   7   12   15   25   27   29   33

5 Which number is a multiple of both 6 and 8? Circle the correct number.

  2   12   14   16   36   40   68   72

6 Which of these numbers is the highest common factor (HCF) of 18 and 27? Circle the correct number.

  2   3   5   7   9   17   45   54

Calculations

7 Add together 1084, 263 and 3146.

_____

8 Subtract 78 from 241.

_____

9 During the day the temperature was 4°C. At night it was -3°C. What was the difference between the two temperatures?

_____ °C

10 Calculate 6×8

_____

11 Which of these numbers is the remainder when you divide 37 by 5? Circle the correct number.

  1   2   3   4   5   7

12 Calculate $484 \div 4$

_____

Mark

13 Look at this torn off shopping bill. If you buy all these items, how much change will you get from £20?

```
Semi-skimmed milk    £0.86
Mushrooms            £0.99
Bananas              £0.69
Meat                 £2.95
Carrots              £1.89
```

£ _____

14 Last year, Class 6F earned 84 house points in total.
There are four houses in the school: Green, Blue, Red and Yellow.
Pupils in Yellow house earned 24 points, pupils in Blue house
earned 36 points and pupils in Green house earned 14 points.
How many points did pupils in Red house earn?

_____

15 I think of a number, multiply it by 3 and subtract 7. My answer is 20.
What is the number I am thinking of?

_____

16 What is the value of x in the equation $3x + 3 = 18$?

_____

Fractions, decimals and percentages

17 Which of these fractions is closest to $\frac{1}{4}$? Circle the correct letter.

A $\frac{1}{2}$ **B** $\frac{4}{8}$ **C** $\frac{3}{4}$ **D** $\frac{5}{16}$ **E** $\frac{3}{8}$

18 Which fraction is biggest? Circle the correct letter.

A $\frac{1}{4}$ **B** $\frac{1}{2}$ **C** $\frac{4}{12}$ **D** $\frac{1}{36}$ **E** $\frac{3}{9}$

19 There are 20 girls in Form 6. 15 of them buy tickets for the
school disco. What fraction of the girls in the class buy tickets?
Give your answer as a fraction in its lowest terms.

_____

20 Which pair of fractions is equivalent? Circle the correct letter.

A $\frac{2}{3}$ and $\frac{4}{5}$ **B** $\frac{2}{3}$ and $\frac{1}{4}$ **C** $\frac{2}{3}$ and $\frac{6}{9}$ **D** $\frac{2}{3}$ and $\frac{4}{9}$ **E** $\frac{1}{4}$ and $\frac{4}{8}$

21 Add together 17.6 and 0.83

_____

22 Calculate 18.4 − 3.8

_____

23 Write $\frac{3}{4}$ as a decimal.

_____

24 Which of these fractions is equivalent to 25%?
Circle the correct letter.

A $\frac{5}{25}$ **B** $\frac{1}{2}$ **C** $\frac{1}{4}$ **D** $\frac{1}{25}$ **E** $\frac{4}{20}$

2

Mark

25 Which of these calculations would you use to find 35% of 250?
Circle the correct letter.

A 35×250 **B** $\dfrac{35 \times 250}{100}$ **C** $\dfrac{35 \times 100}{250}$ **D** $\dfrac{250 \times 100}{35}$ **E** $250 \div 35$

26 There are 25 pupils in Class 6B. 15 pupils in this class are girls.
What percentage is this?   _____ %

27 There are 24 pupils in Class 6C. 16 pupils in this class are boys.
What is the ratio of boys to girls in its simplest form?
_____

28 A car uses 15 litres of petrol on a journey of 180km.
At the same rate, how many litres of petrol will the
car use on a journey of 120km?   _____

Working with charts and data

The children in Form 6 were asked to choose their favourite fruits.
The results were displayed on the bar chart below.

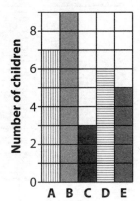

A: Banana
B: Apple
C: Orange
D: Grape
E: Pear

29 How many children chose apple as their favourite fruit?   _____

30 How many children took part in the above survey?   _____

31 Here are Tom's scores in his last 7 spelling tests.

3 8 7 5 9 8 6

What is the range of his scores? Circle the correct letter.

A 3   **B** 6   **C** 8   **D** 9   **E** 46

32 Here are some scores in a recent test.

4 8 18 16 13 16

Which of these numbers represents the modal score? Circle the correct letter.

A 14   **B** 15   **C** 16   **D** 18   **E** 75

Mark

33 You have a set of ten cards numbered 1 to 10. What is the probability of picking a card, at random, which is a factor of 12? Circle the correct letter.

A 40% **B** 25% **C** 60% **D** 75% **E** 50%

34 What is the probability of throwing a six (6) with a normal dice? Circle the correct letter.

A Impossible **B** Possible **C** Very likely **D** Certain **E** Even chance

Shape and space

Look at the line of shapes below.

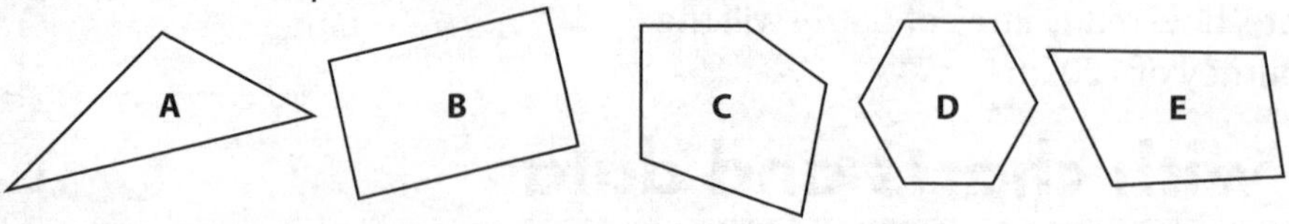

35 Which is the regular shape? _____

36 Which of the shapes above has only 2 lines of symmetry? _____

37 Estimate the size of angle a. Circle the correct letter.

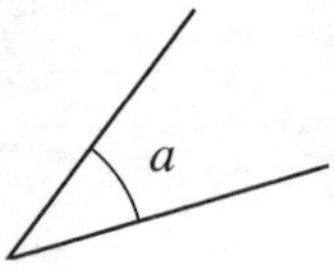

A 10° **B** 30° **C** 50° **D** 70° **E** 90°

38 Complete this statement:
'The angles in a quadrilateral add up to _____ degrees.'

39 A rectangle has length 7cm and width 4cm. What is its perimeter? Circle the correct letter.

A 3cm **B** 11cm **C** 18cm **D** 22cm **E** 28cm

40 One side of a square has length 4cm.
What is the area of the square? _____ cm²

4

Look at the coordinate diagram below.

Mark

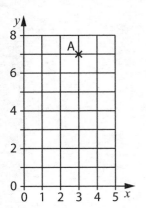

41 What are the coordinates of A?   (____ , ____)

42 On the same grid mark the points **B** (3 , 1), **C** (1 , 1) and **D** (1 , 7).
    Draw a straight line from **A** to B, **B** to C, **C** to **D** and **D** to A.

43 Reflect the shaded shape in the mirror line.

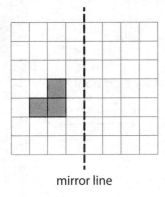

mirror line

44 This shape is moved 3 squares to the right, 1 square down.
    Draw its new position on the grid.

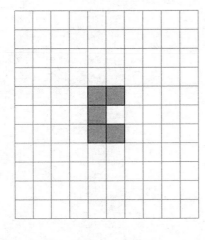

Practice test 1

5

Mark

45 Draw the missing pattern in this sequence of dots.

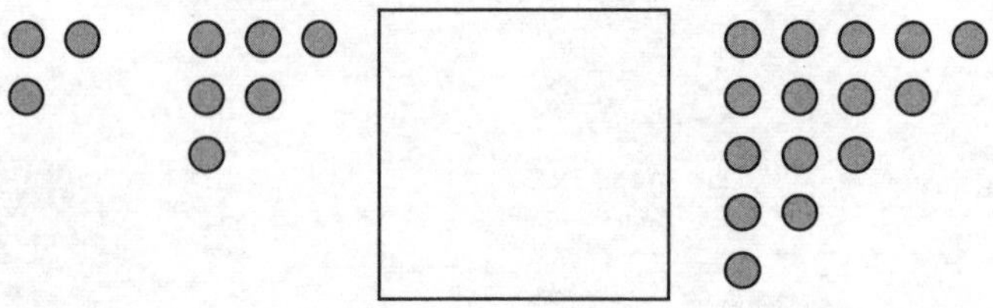

46 These shapes are made up of squares.

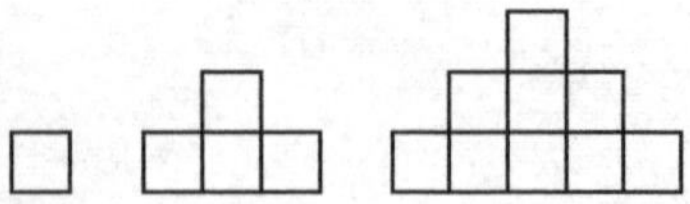

How many squares would you need to build this shape?

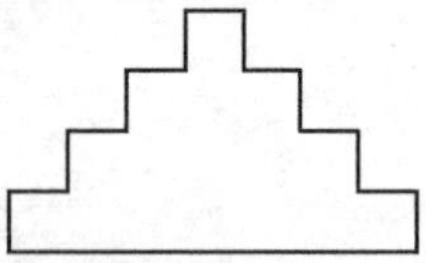

_____

Measuring

47 Which of these containers could hold about 5 litres of water when full?
Circle the correct letter.

   A Teaspoon   **B** Washing up bowl   **C** Teacup   **D** Bath   **E** Swimming pool

48 How many milligrams (mg) are there in 30 grams?   _____ mg

49 It takes Zoe 25 minutes to walk from home to the shops.
She leaves home at 8.45am

What time should she get to the shops?   _____

50 How many days are there in the month of June? Circle the correct letter.

   A 12   **B** 29   **C** 30   **D** 31   **E** 28

Write your answers on the lines provided. When you are given a choice of answers, you will need to circle the letter (A, B, C, D or E) you think is correct. Some questions ask you to mark a diagram. Please use an extra sheet of paper for your workings. *Do not write answers in the 'Mark' column.*

You may not use a calculator.

Numbers and their properties

Mark

1 Round 235 to the nearest 10. _____

2 What is the value of the digit 7 in the number 6723? Circle the correct letter.

   A Seventy   **B** Seven thousand   **C** Seven   **D** Seven hundred   **E** Seventy-two

3 Write these temperatures in order of size, starting with the lowest.

   -6°C   4°C   -3°C   5°C   0°C   -4°C   3°C   7°C

   ____°C ____°C ____°C ____°C ____°C ____°C ____°C ____°C

4 What is the 6th term in the number series beginning 1, 4, 9, 16…? _____

5 These numbers make up a common number pattern.

   1   3   6   10   15   21   28   36   45   55

   What are these numbers called? _____ numbers

6 What is the lowest common multiple (LCM) of both 6 and 9? Circle the correct letter.

   A 54   **B** 18   **C** 15   **D** 3   **E** 1

7 Which of these is a factor of 57? Circle the correct letter.

   A 3   **B** 5   **C** 6   **D** 7   **E** 114

Calculations

8 Add together 196, 29, 261 and 475. _____

9 Subtract 178 from 324. _____

10 The temperature during a winter's day was 2 °C.
   At night the temperature was 5 °C lower.
   What was the night-time temperature? _____ °C

11 What is 18^4? Circle the correct letter.

   A 18×4 **B** $18 \times 18 \times 18 \times 18$ **C** $18 + 4$ **D** $18 \div 4$ **E** $18 + 18 + 18 + 18$

12 Calculate $208 \div 16$ _____

Practice test 2

Mark

13 Find the square root of 49. _____

14 Five pens cost 85p. What is the cost of three pens? _____ p

15 Mena is going on a holiday which will cost £482.
She has already paid a deposit of £50.
The rest of the money will be paid in 8 equal amounts each month.
How much will Mena have to pay each month? £ _____

16 What is the value of p in the equation $2p + r = s$ when $r = 6$ and $s = 14$? _____

17 Tim delivers 150 papers and is paid 20p for each paper.
Use this formula to work out how much he is paid altogether. £ _____

total pay = payment for one paper × number of papers

Fractions, decimals and percentages

18 Write $3\frac{3}{4}$ as an improper fraction. _____

19 In a survey of 63 pupils, $\frac{4}{7}$ of them said that
their favourite colour was green. How many pupils
chose green as their favourite colour? _____

20 Calculate $\frac{3}{4}$ of 56. _____

21 Subtract 4.86 from 17.42 _____

22 Put these decimal numbers in order of size, starting with the smallest.

0.31   0.47   0.5   0.306

_____   _____   _____   _____

smallest   ➔   ➔   *largest*

23 What fraction is equivalent to 45%?
Give your answer in its lowest terms. _____

24 What percentage is equivalent to 0.18? Circle the correct letter.

A 180%   **B** 1.8%   **C** 82%   **D** 0.18%   **E** 18%

25 A full packet contains 10 cakes. Six cakes have been eaten.
What percentage is this? _____ %

26 There are 380 pupils in a school.
On Monday 35% of them have school dinners.
How many pupils have a school dinner that day? _____

8

27 On a map the distance between two villages is 10cm.
The scale of the map is 1cm : 25 000cm.
What is the actual distance between the two villages? Circle the correct letter.

A 2.5km **B** 25km **C** 250km **D** 2500km **E** 25 000km

28 In a test the ratio of correct to incorrect answers for one question was 4 : 5.
There were 63 answers altogether for this question.
How many answers were correct?

Working with charts and data

This pie chart shows the type of book chosen by 24 pupils from the school library.

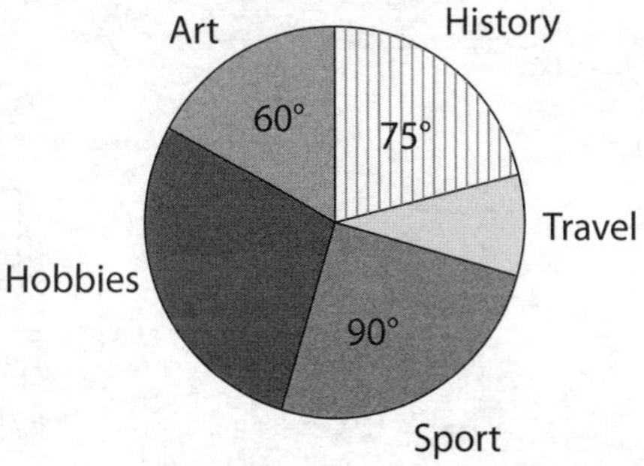

29 How many pupils chose a book about Art?

30 Two pupils chose a book about travel.
What angle represents this amount on the pie chart? _____ °

31 Here are the ages of members of Highcliffe canoe club.

19   16   17   12   19   18   16   15   17   16

What is the median age of club members?

32 Ten children from the local youth club took part in a Swimathon
to raise money for charity. Here are the number of lengths they completed.

13   23   30   8   16   15   34   4   8   9

What is the mean number of lengths? Circle the correct letter.

A 30 **B** 14 **C** 16 **D** 8 **E** 160

33 A seven-sided spinner is equally likely to land on any of the numbers from 1 to 7.
What is the probability of the spinner landing on an odd number?
Circle the correct letter.

A $\frac{2}{7}$ **B** $\frac{3}{7}$ **C** $\frac{4}{7}$ **D** $\frac{5}{7}$ **E** $\frac{7}{7}$

34 A bag contains 5 blue and 3 white counters. A counter is taken from
the bag at random. What is the probability that the counter taken
out will be a white one? Give your answer as a fraction.

Mark

Shape and space

Mark

35 What shape is each face of a cube? Circle the correct letter.

A Circular   **B** Rectangular   **C** Square   **D** Triangular   **E** Cuboid

36 Which of these shapes is the net of a cube. Circle the correct letter.

A   **B**   **C**   **D**   **E**

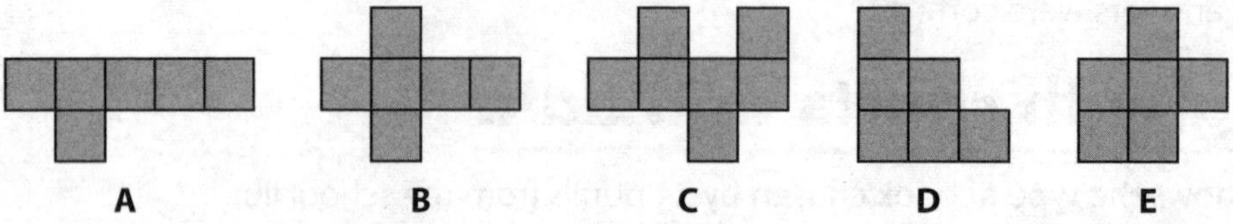

37 What is the size of angle a in this diagram?

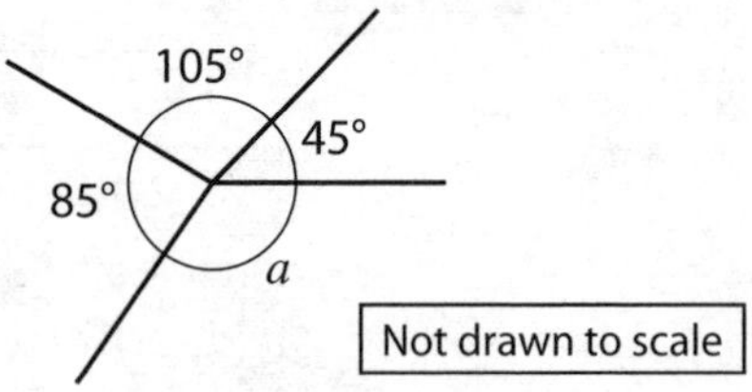

105°

45°

85°

a

Not drawn to scale

_____ °

38 Complete the statement:

'The interior angles of a triangle total _____ °'

39 Look at this shape.

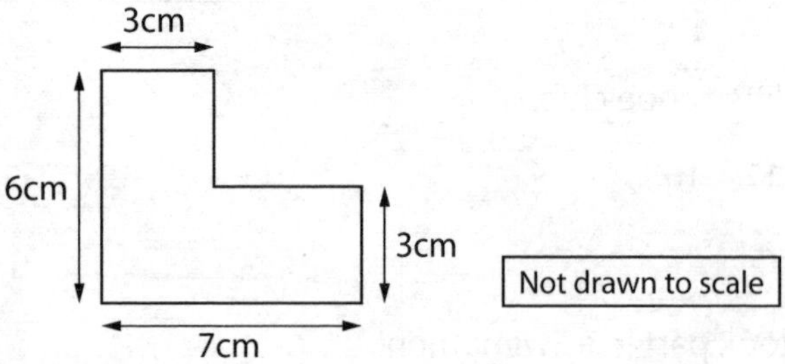

3cm

6cm

3cm

7cm

Not drawn to scale

What is the perimeter of the shape?   _____ cm

40 Find the volume of this cuboid in cubic centimetres.

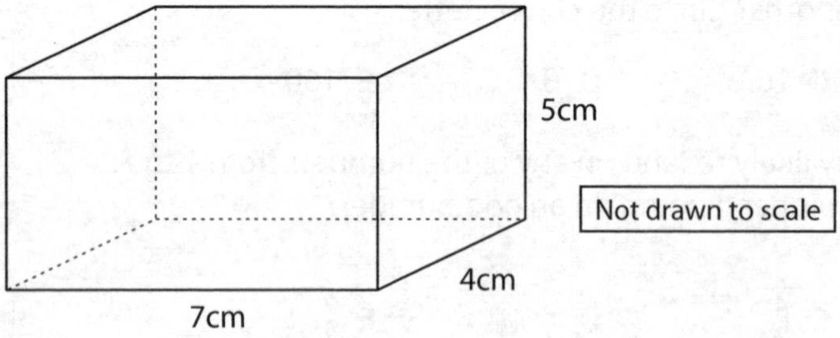

5cm

Not drawn to scale

4cm

7cm

_____ cm³

10

Look at this coordinate diagram.

Mark

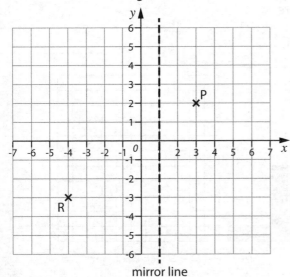

mirror line

41 What are the coordinates of point P? Circle the correct letter.

A (2, 3) **B** (3, 2) **C** (-3, 2) **D** (-2, 3) **E** (2, 2)

☐

42 What are the coordinates of point R? (___ , ___)

☐

43 Point R is reflected in the mirror line. Mark the reflection of R on the diagram above.

☐

44 The arrow is rotated clockwise through 90° about point X.
Find its new position. Circle the correct letter.

A **B** **C** **D** **E**

☐

45 Which set of instructions will guide the explorer (E) through the jungle,
and back to his plane (P)? Circle the correct letter.

A Forward 5, turn right 90°, forward 3,
turn left 90°, forward 3, turn left 90°,
forward 1, turn right 90°, forward 7,
turn right 90°, forward 4

B Forward 5, turn left 90°, forward 3,
turn left 90°, forward 9,
turn right 90°, forward 4

C Forward 5, turn left 90°, forward 3,
turn right 90°, forward 10, forward 4

D Forward 5, turn left 90°, forward 3,
turn right 90°, forward 9,
turn left 90°, forward 4

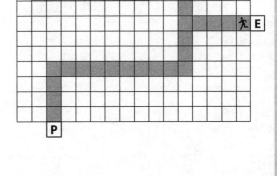

E Forward 5, turn right 90°, forward 3, turn right 90°, forward 9, turn left 90°, forward 4

☐

Practice test 2

Mark

46 Look at this sequence of shapes made from squares. How many squares are there in the 6th member of this sequence? You may use the grid to draw the pattern.

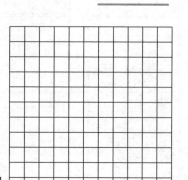

Measuring

47 A beaker holds 250ml of juice. How many beakers can be filled using $2\frac{1}{2}$ litres of juice? Circle the correct letter.

A 4   **B** 8   **C** 10   **D** 12   **E** 20

48 Gracie's house is about 5km from the nearest cinema. Approximately how many miles is this? Circle the correct letter.

A 50 miles   **B** 5 miles   **C** 8 miles   **D** 10 miles   **E** 3 miles

49 Write 2.35pm in 24-hour clock time.

50 It takes Conor a quarter of an hour to cycle from his home to the skateboard park. He leaves home at 15.55 and stops on the way at a friend's house for 25 minutes. At what time will he get to the skateboard park?

Follow the instructions on page 10 to give this test.

1   What is twenty-five to the nearest ten?

2   Write in figures the number one hundred thousand and two.

3   Write two multiples of eight between 50 and 70.

4   Find the total of eighty-three, seventeen and thirty-one.

5   Subtract thirty-three from one hundred and fifty.

6   Multiply thirty six by three.

7   Divide four thousand by two hundred and fifty.

8   What is eleven squared plus two squared?

9   If five y equals forty, what is the value of y?

10   If fifty-six pounds are shared equally between seven friends, how much will each friend receive?

11   What is one and two-thirds as an improper fraction?

12   Find the sum of one point six, two point four and four.

13   Write three-fifths as a percentage.

14   On Monday fifty-six percent of the school were absent. What percentage was present?

15   For every five red fish there are two green fish. If you have twenty red fish, how many green fish will there be?

16   Look at the numbers on your answer sheet: three, six, seven, two, nine, two, one, two. What is the mode of these numbers?

17   If you have nine blue marbles and three green marbles in a bag, what is the probability of picking out a blue marble?

18   How many faces does an octagonal prism have?

19   How many degrees do the internal angles of a square add up to?

20   If one side of a regular pentagon is four centimetres long, what is its perimeter?

21   If one side of a square measures nine centimetres, what is the area?

22   What number is indicated on the scale? *Note: this scale is reproduced on the answer sheet.*

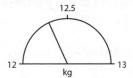

23   What is a quarter of eighty-four litres?

24   What is three kilograms in grams?

25   How many minutes in two and a quarter hours?

Mental maths test 2

Follow the instructions on page 10 to give this test.

1. What is five hundred and fifty-five to the nearest ten?

2. Write in figures the number one thousand and three.

3. Write two prime numbers between 50 and 60.

4. Find the total of eighty-seven, thirteen and thirty-one.

5. Subtract fifteen from ninety-three.

6. Multiply eighty-seven by two.

7. Divide three hundred and twenty-four by three.

8. What is the square root of forty-nine plus the square root of sixteen?

9. If six y plus two is thirty-eight, what is the value of y?

10. If thirty-two pounds are shared equally between four friends, how much will each friend receive?

11. What is two-thirds of thirty-three?

12. Find the sum of one point six two, two point nine and five.

13. Write five twentieths as a percentage.

14. If an eight centimetre plant grows by one hundred and fifty percent during the summer what is the new size of the plant?

15. For every seven red apples there are two green apples. If there are twenty-one red apples, how many green apples are there?

16. Look at the numbers on your answer sheet: three, three, six, seven, two, nine, two, one, two. What is the median of these numbers?

17. If you have nine blue marbles, one red marble and three green marbles in a bag, what is the probability of picking out a white marble?

18. How many vertices does a heptagonal prism have?

19. How many degrees do the internal angles of a parallelogram add up to?

20. If one side of a regular octagon is seven centimetres long, what is its perimeter?

21. If one side of a square measures eleven metres, what is the area?

22. What number is indicated on the scale? *Note: this scale is reproduced on the answer sheet.*

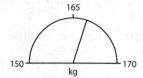

23. How many millilitres are there in two and a quarter litres?

24. What is five point six kilograms in grams?

25. How many minutes between five past three in the afternoon and four thirty pm?

Question	Answer	Jottings	Mark
1			
2			
3			
4			
5			
6			
7			
8			
9	$y =$		
10	£		
11			
12			
13	%		
14	%		
15			
16		3 6 7 2 9 2 1 2	
17			
18			
19	°		
20			
21			
22			
23	l		
24	g		
25			

Mental maths test 1 answer sheet

Mental maths test 2 answer sheet

Question	Answer	Jottings	Mark
1			
2			
3			
4			
5			
6			
7			
8			
9	$y =$		
10	£		
11			
12			
13	%		
14			
15			
16		3 3 6 7 2 9 2 1 2	
17			
18			
19	°		
20			
21			
22			
23	ml		
24	g		
25			

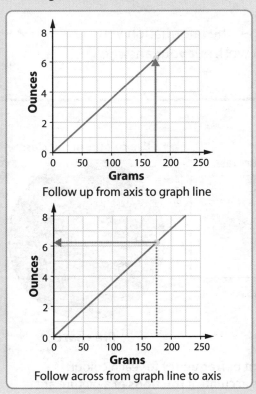

This conversion graph shows that 175 grams is the same as 6.2 ounces.

Follow up from axis to graph line

Follow across from graph line to axis

TIPS FOR SUCCESS

Scales

It's important to read the axis scales carefully, especially with line and conversion graphs, as a misread will lead to a wrong answer.

Pie charts

Make sure you know that there are 360° in a pie chart (circle). Each half (semicircle) equals 180° and each quarter equals 90°. These facts will help you answer lots of questions about pie charts.

What you will learn

In this section you will learn about these data topics:

- charts and graphs
- finding the mode, median, mean and range
- probability.

2   You often have to reason about the data, rather than just applying a set method to calculate something.

If four numbers are 6, 5, 7 and x, and their mean is 6, what is x?

If the mean of four numbers is 6, then they must total 24. The three numbers you know add up to 18, so x must be 6.

3   Probabilities are fractions, so you often need to find a total and express one of the numbers as a fraction of this.

If you pick a sweet at random out of a bag containing 5 chocolates and 15 fruity sweets, the probability of getting a chocolate is $\frac{1}{4}$.

There are 5 + 15 = 20 sweets in the bag, so the chocolates are $\frac{5}{20}$ or $\frac{1}{4}$ of them.

In the test, you can expect to find questions like this.

- In a survey of class 6H, 18 people had dark hair, 9 had fair hair and 3 had ginger hair. On a pie chart to show this information, what angle would represent the people with fair hair?

  A 9°   **B** 12°   **C** 36°   **D** 108°   **E** 180°

  There are 18 + 9 + 3 = 30 people in the class, so one person will be represented by 360° ÷ 30 = 12°. 12° × 9 = 108°, so the correct answer is D.

- Using the conversion graph above, how many grams is equal to 4 ounces? Give your answer correct to the nearest 10 grams.

  Working across from 4 on the ounces axis and then down to the grams axis gives a value that is not quite halfway between 100g and 125g. Halfway would be 112.5g, so the reading is about 110g.

Charts and graphs

Charts and graphs are ways of displaying information in a pictorial way, either to make it easier to understand, or to make an impact.

The skill you need to practise is being able to get the information you need from a chart or graph quickly, so you can work out your answer.

Understanding charts

These charts all display the same information.

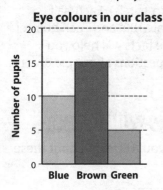

Bar chart

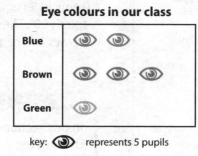

key: represents 5 pupils

Pictogram

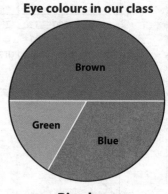

Pie chart

The bar chart makes it easy to compare the amount or **frequency** for each colour. The pictogram displays this clearly, but can be less accurate if **fractions** of a picture are shown. The **pie chart** is good for showing fractions of the whole.

Understanding graphs

The graphs you may find in your question paper fall into two main types:

- **time-based graphs**
- **conversion graphs**.

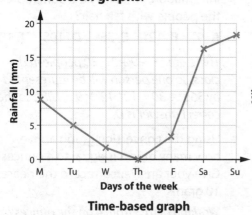

Time-based graph

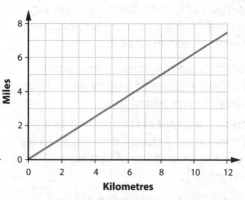

Conversion graph

A time-based graph shows how something develops over time. The time units could be anything from seconds to years. A conversion graph shows a relationship between two amounts – a straight line shows that the amounts are in **proportion**.

Chart and graph skills

Reading information

The most basic skill is finding information from a chart or graph. Here are some examples from the charts and graphs on the previous page.

Bar chart or pictogram: how many pupils have green eyes?   *5 pupils*

Pie chart: what fraction have brown eyes? $\frac{1}{2}$

Time-based graph: Which day of the week was dry?   *Thursday (rainfall = 0)*

Working with information

You may be asked to find information from a chart or graph and then perform a basic calculation with it. Here are some examples from the charts and graphs opposite.

Bar chart: how many pupils were there in the class?   *10 + 15 + 5 = 30*

Pie chart: how many pupils out of 30 have brown eyes?

30 ÷ 2 = 15 pupils ($\frac{1}{2}$ is shaded so find $\frac{1}{2}$ of 30)

or 360º ÷ 180º = 2 and 30 ÷ 2 = 15

Conversion graph: how many miles is the same as 80km?

Read off the graph that 8km = 5 miles, and multiply by 10 to get 50 miles.

Solving problems with charts and graphs

1   In this question you have to calculate using information from a bar chart.

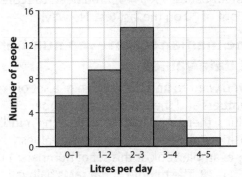

- In a survey, people were asked how much water they drank in a day on average. The bar chart shows the results.

How many people drank 3 litres or less?
Add together the figures for 0–1, 1–2 and 2–3 litres → 6 + 9 + 14 = 29 people.

2   In this question you have to calculate using information from a graph.

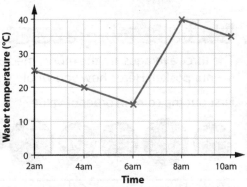

- The graph shows the temperature of water in a water tank. What is the difference between the maximum and minimum temperature?

The maximum is 40°C and the minimum is 15°C. The difference is 40 – 15 = 25°C

TEST YOURSELF

1   The pictogram shows the results of a survey. How many people preferred music?

Favourite arts subject in school

2   The graph converts weights in kilograms to pounds. How many pounds is 1.5kg?

   A 0.6

   B 0.7

   C 1.1

   D 2.2

   E 3.3

The mode, median, mean and range are examples of statistics. Statistics are numbers that give you information about a set of data.

The **mode**, **median** and **mean** are types of average. They are representative of a set of data in some way. The **range** is completely different – it tells you how 'spread out' the set of data is. Remember that the word **frequency** means the number of times a value occurs in a set of data.

Understanding averages and range

The three averages are the mode, median and mean. Suppose you found this change in your pocket. Here's how you would work out the three averages.

First put the coins in order of value.

Mode	The most common value	The frequencies are 4 × 1p, 3 × 2p, 1 × 5p, 2 × 10p, 1 × 20p. There are more 1p coins than any of the others, so 1p is the mode.
Median	The middle value	Arrange the coins in order of value: 1 1 1 1 2 ② 2 5 10 10 20 The one in the middle of the list is a 2, so 2p is the median.
Mean	Total value divided by total frequency	The total value of the change is 55p. There are 11 coins, so the mean is 55 ÷ 11 = 5p. This is the mean value of a coin in this set of change.

The range is not an average – it is the difference between the smallest and largest values in the data.

For the coins, the range is 20 – 1 = 19p

…if you've ever lined up with your class in order of height, the person in the middle has the median height.

Statistical skills

Before beginning questions associated with the mode, median, mean and range, it is helpful to put the numbers you are going to work with in **ascending order**. This includes repeated numbers.

'Working backwards' with the mean

Suppose your mean mark out of 10 for four Maths tests is 8. There is one more test to come and you need to get a mean score of 9 to beat your friend. Can you do it? If your mean so far is 8, your total is 8 × 4 = 32

To get a mean of 9 on 5 tests, your total score must be 9 × 5 = 45. You need to score 13 out of 10 on the last test. No way!

The median for an even number of data values

If you want to find the median of a set of numbers and there is an even number of values, there is no middle value – the middle position falls between two of the values. For example, look at this set of numbers: 11, 14, 17, 18. The middle of the set is halfway between 14 and 17, so you find the number halfway between them – $15\frac{1}{2}$ or 15.5

Averages from a frequency table or chart

Sometimes you may be given data as a frequency table (or in a bar chart, which amounts to the same thing). Look at this survey of shoe sizes in a class.

Shoe size	5	6	7	8
Frequency	2	7	10	5

The mode is obviously 7 as it occurs 10 times, i.e. more than any other shoe size.

The total frequency (the number of people in the class) = 2 + 7 + 10 + 5 = 24, so the median is halfway between the 12th and 13th value. These are both 7, so the median is 7.

To 'add up' all the shoe sizes, multiply each shoe size by its frequency, then find the sum of these.

$(5 \times 2) + (6 \times 7) + (7 \times 10) + (8 \times 5) = 10 + 42 + 70 + 40 = 162$

$162 \div 24 = 6.75$ so this is the mean.

Solving problems with averages and the range

1 In this question you have to compare two sets of data.

- The pupils in two classes were asked how many brothers and sisters they had. The tables show the results.

Year 5

1	1	0	2	2	1	1	5	1	0
1	0	0	1	4	1	0	2	2	0

Year 6

2	1	0	2	3	1	1	3	1	1
0	1	3	1	0	2	2	0	2	0

Which class has more brothers and sisters, on average?

In each class, there are 20 pupils.

The total for Year 5 is 25, so the mean is 25 ÷ 20 = 1.25

The total for Year 5 is 26, so the mean is 26 ÷ 20 = 1.3

So the average number of brothers and sisters is very slightly higher in Year 6.

(Notice that the modes and medians are all 1, so you can't use these averages to help you decide.)

2 In this question you need to 'work backwards' using the median.

- The median of a set of positive whole numbers is 5. The numbers are 5, 8, 1, 6 and x. How many different values of x are possible?

The numbers have to be put in order.

If 5 is the median, two of them will be greater than 5 and two will be smaller. Because 6 and 8 are greater than 5, this means that x must be less than 5. 1 is the smallest positive whole number, so x can't be less than 1.

So the order is 1, x, 5, 6, 8. Therefore x could be 1, 2, 3, 4 or 5.

The answer is that there are 5 possible values.

TEST YOURSELF

1 The table shows the number of merit points scored in a class during the 12 weeks of term.

Merit points

6	5	6	8	10	7	6	7	10	3	10	6

What was the mean number of merit points per week that term?

2 Find the median number of merit points.

3 What was the modal number of merit points?

4 What was the range of the data?

   A 3   **B** 6.5   **C** 7

   D 12   **E** 84

Probability

Probability is a measurement or estimate of how likely something is to happen.

A **probability** is a number between 0 and 1. You can write probabilities as **fractions**, **decimals** or **percentages**. In the test never use language such as '1 in 5' or '5 to 1' – use $\frac{1}{5}$, 0.2 or 20%.

Understanding probability

Things that happen by chance are called events. *Example:* flip a coin.

The possible results of an event are called its **outcomes**. *Example:* head, tail.

Each outcome of an event has a probability. *Example:* probability of a head = $\frac{1}{2}$, probability of a tail = $\frac{1}{2}$.

If all the outcomes have the same probability, they are equally likely.

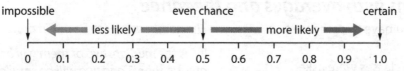

The probability scale is a number line starting at 0 and finishing at 1.

…so when you think about how risky something is before you do it, you are estimating probability.

Probability skills

Calculating a probability

If all the outcomes are equally likely, calculating a probability is straightforward. Just divide the number of desired outcomes by the total number of outcomes.

Example: When you roll an ordinary dice, what is the probability of getting a score that is a **prime number**? There are 6 possible outcomes (1, 2, 3, 4, 5, 6), and 3 of these are prime numbers (2, 3, 5). So the probability is $\frac{3}{6}$ or $\frac{1}{2}$.

Sometimes you can't calculate a probability mathematically in this way, but you can use experiments or trials to help you.

Example: Suppose you dropped a drawing pin on to a table 100 times, and it landed point-up 35 times. You could estimate the probability of it landing point-up as $\frac{35}{100}$ = 0.35 or 35% or $\frac{7}{20}$.

Probabilities adding to one

The probability that an outcome will happen and the probability it will not happen always add up to 1. So if the probability that Jayne misses her bus in the morning is 0.15, the probability that she catches it is 0.85, because 0.15 + 0.85 = 1

Expected frequency

You can use probabilities to calculate an estimate of how many times an outcome will happen. This is called the expected frequency.

Suppose Jayne uses her bus service 200 days each year. She would expect to miss the bus 0.15 × 200 = 30 times.
Note: this is not exact – it is just an estimate.

Solving problems with probability

1 In this question you have to calculate a probability from the information given.

- A bag contains 2 black counters, 2 red counters, 3 blue counters and 5 white counters. Jack takes a counter out of the bag at random. What is the probability he will get a blue counter?

The first thing you need to know is how many counters there are in the bag altogether.

2 + 2 + 3 + 5 = 12

The number of blue counters is 3, so the probability is $\frac{3}{12}$ or $\frac{1}{4}$.

2 Here you need to estimate a probability from some experimental data.

- Masud works in a CD factory. Part of his job is to check the quality of the discs. He tests 500 discs and finds that 25 of them are faulty. What is the probability that a disc chosen at random will not be faulty?

There are two ways to tackle this question.

First method: There were 25 faulty discs out of a total of 500. The probability of finding a faulty disc is $\frac{25}{500} = \frac{1}{20}$. So the probability of picking a 'good' disc at random is $1 - \frac{1}{20} = \frac{19}{20}$

Second method: In Masud's sample, there were 500 − 25 = 475 'good' discs, so the probability of selecting a 'good' disc at random is $\frac{475}{500} = \frac{19}{20}$

1 This spinner is equally likely to land on any of the numbers 1, 4, 9, 16 or 25.

What is the probability that it will land on an odd number?

2 This bar chart shows the results of a survey of eye colours.

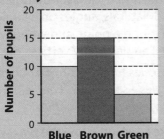

Eye colours in our class

What is the probability that a pupil chosen at random from this class will have blue eyes?

A $\frac{1}{10}$ **B** $\frac{1}{6}$ **C** 30%

D $\frac{1}{3}$ **E** 0.5

3 The probability that a packet of Golden Crunch crisps will contain a free gift is $\frac{1}{6}$. Samantha's Mum buys a multipack with 24 packets in it. How many gifts can Samantha expect to find in the multipack?

Double dice

In board games you often have to roll two dice to move. Try rolling two dice a large number of times and record what scores you get in a tally chart. Use your figures to estimate the probability of getting the different possible scores. Are they all about the same, or is there a most likely score?

Shape and space is the part of Maths that deals with shapes in two dimensions (2-D) and three dimensions (3-D), including their areas, volumes and symmetry. It also includes position (coordinates) and transformations (reflections, rotations and translations).

The properties of 2-D shapes depend on their measurements and the angles they contain. 3-D shapes are built up from 2-D shapes in various ways.

What to expect

There is a huge range of possible questions to do with shape and space. They range from calculations of area and volume to finding unknown sides and angles, carrying out transformations of the shapes and identifying the kinds of symmetry they have.

Coordinate-based questions may just ask you to identify coordinates, or may be more involved, such as looking at the way straight lines on the coordinate grid are related to each other or locating the missing vertex of a shape.

Some questions in the test papers may be multiple-choice. To answer them, you need to select the correct answer from the choices given. Sometimes the choices may be simple answers such as an angle, the name of a shape or a pair of coordinates. Other questions may expect you to decide which of a set of statements is true.

Shape and space skills

One thing that can make shape and space questions difficult is that there are a lot of facts to remember. You can 'reconstruct' most of these if you can't quite remember them, but this takes up valuable time in the test.

1   You need to memorise the names of the different polygons, and any special types:

   Triangles: scalene, isosceles, equilateral

   Quadrilaterals: kite, trapezium, parallelogram, rhombus, rectangle, square

   Pentagon, hexagon, heptagon, octagon, nonagon, decagon…

2   The main angle facts you need to know are the angle sums for triangles and quadrilaterals, angles on a straight line and round a point, and where you find equal angles at the vertices of shapes.

   Isosceles triangles have a pair of equal angles – so do kites. Parallelograms have two pairs of equal angles.

3   Make sure you know the two symmetry types: **reflective** and **rotational**.

   Shapes with reflective symmetry may not have rotational symmetry, and vice versa.

   A kite has a line of symmetry but no rotational symmetry; a parallelogram has rotational symmetry of order 2, but no lines of symmetry.

Introducing shape and space

4 The *x* coordinate (horizontal) is always written before the *y* coordinate (vertical). This only usually causes a problem when a point is on one of the axes.

The point (4, 0) is on the *x*-axis. (0, 1) is on the *y*-axis.

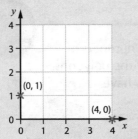

To get from the origin to (4, 0), you move only to the right, which is a horizontal movement, so the y coordinate remains at 0.

For (0, 1), it is a vertical movement only, so the x coordinate remains at 0.

In the test, you can expect to find questions like these.

● What is the side length of a square that has the same area as this triangle?

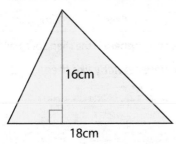

A 17cm **B** 12.5cm **C** 16cm

D 18cm **E** 12cm

The area of the triangle is
$\frac{1}{2} \times 18 \times 16 = 9 \times 16 = 144cm^2$

$12^2 = 144$, *so the correct answer is E.*

TIPS FOR SUCCESS

Areas of triangles and parallelograms

● Make sure you remember that the area of a triangle is *half* the base times the perpendicular height. This is particularly important if you're working backwards from the area to find one of the measurements.

● The area of a parallelogram is the base times the perpendicular height. Don't try to use the length of the other side of the parallelogram, which is sometimes given in the question just to confuse you!

1st

● What is the smallest number of extra squares that need to be coloured so the pattern has two lines of symmetry?

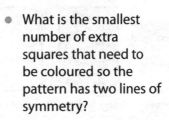

A 4 **B** 6 **C** 8 **D** 10 **E** 12

8 squares is the smallest number so the correct answer is C.

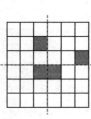

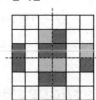

What you will learn

In this section you will learn about these shape and space topics:

● 2-D and 3-D shapes
● angles
● perimeter, area and volume
● coordinates
● reflection, translation and rotation
● patterns and puzzles.

2-D and 3-D shapes *(side tab)*

2-D shapes are flat. A 2-D shape has a boundary made up of lines or curves which separates the inside from the outside. 3-D shapes are solid. A 3-D shape has a boundary made up of flat shapes or curved surfaces.

If a shape has corners, the corners are called **vertices**.
Lines joining vertices are usually called sides in a **2-D shape**, and edges in a **3-D shape**. Flat surfaces on 3-D shapes are called faces.

Understanding shapes

The most common 2-D shapes are **polygons**, with different numbers of straight sides, and circles and semicircles. These are some of the polygons. The numbers inside show how many vertices and sides they have.

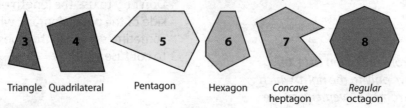

Triangle Quadrilateral Pentagon Hexagon *Concave* heptagon *Regular* octagon

A **concave polygon** has at least one **reflex angle**; a **regular polygon** has equal **angles** and equal sides.

Prisms and **pyramids** are the main types of 3-D shape (or **solid shape**).

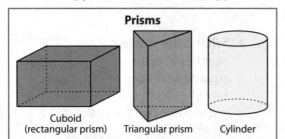

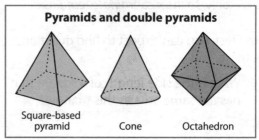

Remember that a **cube** is a special type of **cuboid** with all square faces, and a **sphere** is the shape of a ball.

…lots of objects in real life are very like these shapes, but they're never <u>exactly</u> like them.

Shape skills
Symmetry

Here are some shapes with their **lines of symmetry** drawn. The number shows how many lines of symmetry the shape has.

*A **parallelogram** has no lines of symmetry.*

The order of **rotational symmetry** is the number of positions in which a shape will look the same when rotated.

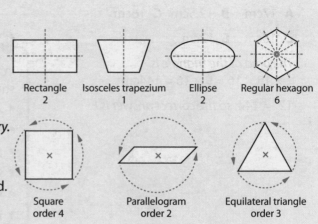

Vertices, faces and edges

You need to know, and be able to retrieve at speed, the properties of common
2-D and 3-D shapes. For example, a cuboid has 8 vertices, 6 faces and 12 edges.

Nets

The **net** of a solid shape can be folded up to make
the shape. It shows all the faces of the shape,
flattened out. This is the net of a triangular prism.

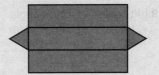

Parts of a circle

You need to know what the parts of a circle are called.
Notice that the **diameter** of a circle is double the **radius**.

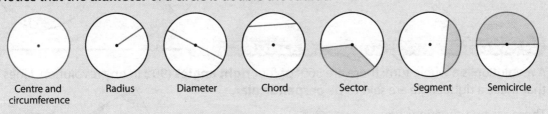

| Centre and circumference | Radius | Diameter | Chord | Sector | Segment | Semicircle |

Solving problems with shapes

1 In this question, you have to find an 'odd
one out' using symmetry.

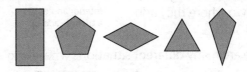

● Which of these shapes has line symmetry
but no rotational symmetry?

*Check that all the shapes have at least one **line of symmetry**. Now find the order of rotational
symmetry for each one: 2, 5, 2, 3… The **kite** has to be rotated all the way before it looks the
same, so this is the correct answer.*

2 This is another 'odd one out' question.

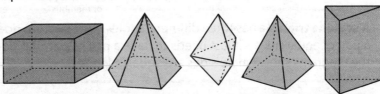

● Two shapes are 'partners'
if they have the same
number of faces.
Which of the five shapes
below has no partner?

*The cube and the double pyramid both have 6 faces. The triangular prism and the square-based
pyramid both have 5, so the hexagonal pyramid (7 faces) has no partner.*

TEST YOURSELF

1 Draw all the lines of
symmetry on this regular
pentagon.

2 This is a net diagram of a
cube. Some edges of the
cube appear twice when it
is drawn as a net diagram.
How many edges of the
cube appear twice in
the diagram?

A 4 **B** 5 **C** 6 **D** 7 **E** 8

An angle is a measure of turning. You find angles wherever straight lines intersect (meet or cross). The angle between two lines is the amount you have to turn one line so it fits on top of the other.

Angles are measured in degrees (°). Angles are given names according to their size.

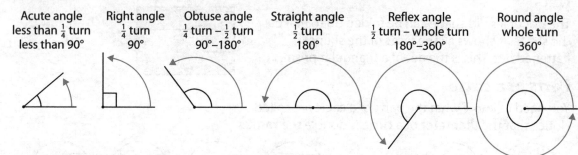

| Acute angle less than ¼ turn less than 90° | Right angle ¼ turn 90° | Obtuse angle ¼ turn – ½ turn 90°–180° | Straight angle ½ turn 180° | Reflex angle ½ turn – whole turn 180°–360° | Round angle whole turn 360° |

Understanding angle relationships

A revolution is a whole turn: there are 360° or four **right angles** (90°) in one revolution. Lines that make a right angle are said to be **perpendicular**.

There are two situations you need to know where angles add up to 180 degrees (°), and two where they add up to 360°.

Interior angles in a triangle add up to 180°

Adjacent angles on a straight line add up to 180°

Interior angles in a quadrilateral add up to 360°

Angles at a point add up to 360°

There are many different situations where angles are equal to each other.

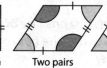
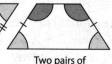

Two angles in an isosceles triangle

All angles in an equilateral triangle (60°)

All angles in a rectangle or square (90°)

Two pairs of opposite angles in a parallelogram or rhombus

Two pairs of adjacent angles in an isosceles trapezium

One pair of opposite angles in a kite

A **scalene triangle** has three different angles. A **trapezium** doesn't have to have a pair of equal sides – it just needs to have a pair of **parallel** sides. The marks on the diagrams show where sides are equal in length.

Angle skills

Finding unknown angles

You may need to use more than one angle relationship to find your answer.

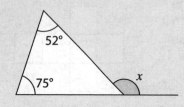

For example, here you need to use the angle sum of a triangle and also **adjacent angles** on a straight line.

The two given angles add up to 127°, so the third angle of the triangle is $180° - 127° = 53°$

This angle is adjacent to x on the line, so $x + 53° = 180°$

x must be 127°

Reasoning with angles

Sometimes you may be given some information and have to use logic to solve the problem. For example, suppose you know that a **parallelogram** contains an angle of 50°. What are the other angles? There must be another 50°, as opposite angles in a parallelogram are equal. That leaves 360° − 100° = 260° for the other two angles, which are also equal, so they must each be 130°.

Estimating angles

You need to be able to look at an angle and get a rough idea what size it is. First decide what type of angle it is (**acute**, **obtuse**, **reflex**). Then it's useful to compare the angle you're trying to estimate with a **multiple** of 45° as these angles are easy to imagine.

Solving problems with angles

1   This is an angle reasoning problem.

● In an isosceles triangle, two of the angles add up to 136°. Which of these *cannot* be an angle of the triangle?

A 72°   **B** 44°   **C** 92°   **D** 68°

It could be that the two equal angles of the triangle add up to 136°. If so, they are each half of 136°, 68°. The other angle is then 44°. If the two angles that add up to 136° are different, the third angle is still 44° and therefore there must be another 44° angle as well. This leaves 180° − 88° = 92° for the other angle. So 72° cannot be an angle of the triangle.

2   This problem is about fitting shapes together.

● Emma has some tiles which are squares and **equilateral triangles**. She puts their **vertices** together to fill up the space around a point. Which of these combinations will *not* fill up the space?

A 4 squares   **B** 3 squares and 2 triangles   **C** 2 squares and 3 triangles   **D** 6 triangles

Add up the angles for each combination.

A $4 \times 90° = 360°$ **B** $3 \times 90° + 2 \times 60° = 390°$ **C** $2 \times 90° + 3 \times 60° = 360°$ **D** $6 \times 60° = 360°$

B's total is over 360°, so there would be an overlap.

TRY IT OUT

Sports pitches

Do an Internet search or use a book to look at the areas on which different sports are played. What shape are they? How are they marked out? What angles can you find?

TEST YOURSELF

1   The diagram shows a **kite**.
Find the size of the angle marked x.

2   Angle e is one **interior angle** of an equilateral triangle.
Which of these statements is not true?

   A $e + 120°$ is a straight angle   **B** e is acute

   C e is $\frac{1}{3}$ of a right angle   **D** e is $\frac{1}{6}$ of a whole turn

   E You could find an angle the same size as e in a **hexagon**

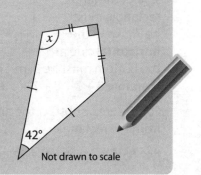

42°

Not drawn to scale

A 2-D shape has a perimeter (the distance all the way around its boundary) and an area (the amount of surface inside its perimeter). A 3-D shape has a surface area (the total area of its boundary) and a volume (the amount of space inside its surface).

Perimeter is measured in length units such as centimetres (cm) or metres (m), and for a **polygon** the perimeter is the sum of the lengths of all its sides. **Area** is measured in units such as square centimetres (cm^2) or square metres (m^2). The units of **volume** are cubic centimetres (cm^3) or cubic metres (m^3). Also, volume units match with **capacity** units: $1cm^3$ is the same as 1 millilitre (ml), so a litre is $1000cm^3$.

Understanding area

Some simple shapes have **formulae** for their areas.

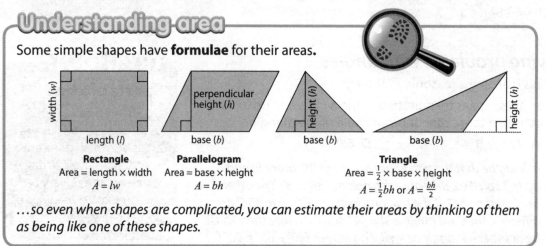

Rectangle
Area = length × width
$A = lw$

Parallelogram
Area = base × height
$A = bh$

Triangle
Area = $\frac{1}{2}$ × base × height
$A = \frac{1}{2}bh$ or $A = \frac{bh}{2}$

…so even when shapes are complicated, you can estimate their areas by thinking of them as being like one of these shapes.

Perimeter and area skills

Compound shapes

Compound shapes are formed when simpler shapes are combined to make something more complicated. Shapes can be added to each other or subtracted. For example, look at this shape, made by subtracting a square from a rectangle.

For the perimeter, notice that the unmarked **vertical** side of the large rectangle must be 7cm and the **horizontal** side at the bottom must be 8cm. The perimeter is therefore 8 + 7 + 8 + 7 + 3 + 3 = 36cm

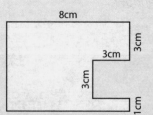

For the area, subtract the area of the square from the rectangle:

$8 \times 7 - 3 \times 3 = 56 - 9 = 47cm^2$

Working backwards

If you know the area of a shape and one of the measurements, you can calculate the other measurement. For example, if the area of a rectangle is $30m^2$ and its width is 3m, the length is 30 ÷ 3 = 10m.

If you have to do this with a triangle, be careful! The area formula contains a factor of $\frac{1}{2}$, so you need to take account of this. If the area of the triangle is $12cm^2$ and the base is 4cm, you know that $\frac{1}{2} \times 4 \times$ height = 12, so 2 × height = 12, so the height must be 6cm.

Changing units

If the measurements are given in different units, you need to change one of them so they match. For example, the area of a rectangle 2cm by 8mm would be $20 \times 8 = 160mm^2$ or $2 \times 0.8 = 1.6cm^2$

Understanding volume and surface area

You need to know these volume formulae.

The **surface area** of a **solid shape** is just the area of its **net**.

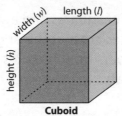

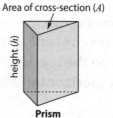

Cuboid
Volume = length × width × height
$V = lwh$

Prism
Volume = area of cross-section × height
$V = Ah$

Volume skills
Calculations

Volume problems are usually straightforward calculations.

Packing problems

You may be asked to work out how many small shapes will fit inside a larger shape. For example, how many 2cm by 3cm by 4cm packs will fit inside a box which is a 12cm **cube**?

12cm = 6 × 2cm,
4 × 3cm and 3 × 4cm,
so the answer is 6 × 4 × 3 = 72 packs.

Solving problems with perimeter, area and volume

1 In this question, you need to change area units.

● The shaded square has area 25mm². What is the area of the whole shape in cm²?

Cartons

Find some **cuboid**-shaped drinks cartons. For each one, measure it and work out its volume. Does the volume match the capacity printed on the pack?

The rectangles are twice the area of the small square, and the large square is twice the area of one of the rectangles, so the total area is 12 times that of the small square. 12 × 25 = 300mm² = 3cm²

2 This is a problem about volume and capacity.

● A fish tank is 40cm by 30cm by 15cm. How many litres of water does it hold when completely full?

40 × 30 = 1200
1200 × 15 = 18 000cm³ = 18 litres

TEST YOURSELF

1 Find the volume of this cuboid in cubic centimetres, and the surface area in square centimetres.

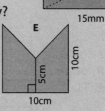

8mm

10mm

15mm

2 Two of these shapes have the same area. Which are they?

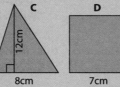

A 6cm 10cm
B 6cm 5cm 15cm
C 12cm 8cm
D 7cm 7cm
E 5cm 10cm 10cm

A B and E **B** A and B **C** C and D **D** C and E **E** A and C

Coordinates

Coordinates are a way of describing the position of an object in two dimensions. Grid references on maps are similar to coordinates.

To use **coordinates**, you need a grid of squares and a starting point called the **origin**. **Axes** containing number scales cross at the origin. You can then identify positions on the grid using the numbers from the axes. The axes are usually labelled x (**horizontal**) and y (**vertical**).

Understanding coordinates

The axes containing number scales divide the coordinate grid into four **quadrants**. In the 1st quadrant, both coordinates are **positive** so points are to the *right* and *up* from the origin. In the diagram, the coordinates of point A are (4, 2). This tells you to move 4 units to the right of the origin and 2 units up.

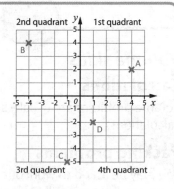

The x coordinate is always written before the y coordinate. Some people use the phrase 'along the corridor before you climb the stairs' to remember this.

Negative coordinates tell you to move *left* or *down* from the origin. The coordinates of the other points on the grid are B (-4, 4), C (-1, -5) and D (1, -2).

Sometimes you will see axes that only show the first quadrant:

Points on the axes will always have coordinates that contain a zero. So point X is (4, 0) and Y is (0, 1).

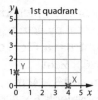

…so when you use a device with a touch screen, the screen is sending coordinate information to the device.

Coordinate skills

Decimal coordinates

You may be asked to state the coordinates of a point where the grid is 'magnified' so that the values are **decimal**. For example, the coordinates of point P are (0.4, 0.7).

Parallel and perpendicular lines

Some questions ask about straight lines drawn on the grid. You may need to identify lines that are **parallel** or **perpendicular**.

In this example, you have to find a line perpendicular to a given line (L), passing through a particular point (T).

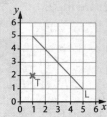

The perpendicular line is shown in blue, and the possible coordinates on this grid are (0, 1), (2, 3), (3, 4), (4, 5) and (5, 6).

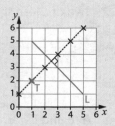

Completing shapes

You need to be able to add points to a grid to produce a given shape. In this example, the idea is to add a **vertex** to produce a right-angled **isosceles triangle**, given the two vertices at A and B.

The blue points are all possible answers.

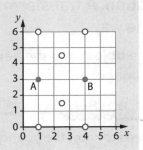

Solving problems with coordinates

1   In this question, you have to identify the coordinates of three points in order.

● What are the coordinates of U, V and W? Choose the correct letter.

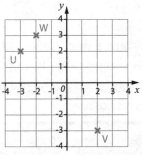

   A U (-3, 2)   V (2, -3)   W (-2, 3)

   B U (2, -3)   V (-3, 2)   W (-2, 3)

   C U (-2, 3)   V (2, -3)   W (-3, 2)

   D U (-2, 3)   V (-3, 2)   W (2, -3)

   E U (-3, 2)   V (2, -3)   W (3, -2)

*The x coordinate of U is negative, so you can rule out **B**. The y coordinate of V is negative, so that rules out **D**. The x coordinate of W is negative, so that rules out **E**, leaving a choice between **A** and **C**. The x coordinate of U in **C** is -2, which is clearly wrong, so the answer is **A**.*

2   In this question, there are points which are halfway between gridlines.

● The map shows the plan of a motorway service area. Which feature is at (3.5, 1.5)?

From the origin, move 3.5 units right and then 1.5 units up. You are at the café.

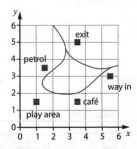

TEST YOURSELF

1   A fourth point D is added to this diagram so that ABCD is a square. What are the coordinates of D?

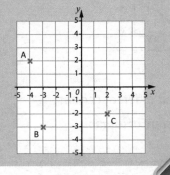

2   The endpoints of five lines are shown below. Which pair of points forms a line parallel to the one in the diagram?

   A (-2, 1) and (2, -1)

   B (-5, 1) and (4, 4)

   C (-4, 0) and (2, 3)

   D (-2, 0) and (3, 0)

   E (2, 2) and (5, 3)

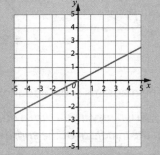

Reflection, translation and rotation

Reflection, translation and rotation are types of mathematical transformation. A transformation takes a shape and alters it in some way.

The original shape is called the **object** and the new shape after the **transformation** is called the **image**.

Understanding reflection

To carry out a **reflection** you need to know the position of the line of reflection or **mirror line**.

 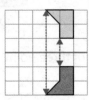 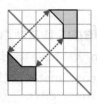 

The diagrams show a shape reflected in different lines. The green arrows show that the **perpendicular** distances of the object and image from the mirror line are equal.

…so when you look in the mirror, the distance from your nose to the mirror is the same as your reflection's nose.

Understanding translation

A **translation** is just a sliding movement. You need to know the amount of **horizontal** and **vertical** movement to describe a translation.

The diagram shows a translation 6 units to the right and 2 units down. You have to be careful to make sure that you pick corresponding (matching) points on the object and image.

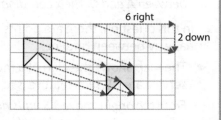

…so when you move the cursor on a computer screen, the computer is separating your mouse movements into horizontal and vertical parts.

Understanding rotation

To carry out a **rotation** you need to know what angle to turn through (say **clockwise** or **anticlockwise** as well to be clear), and, sometimes, where the centre of rotation is.

The diagrams show a triangle rotated 90° anticlockwise about different centres.

…so whenever you turn a door handle it is rotating about its centre of rotation, in the middle or at the end, depending on the type of handle.

Transformation skills

Carry out the transformation

Use the information given to reflect, translate or rotate an object.
You will usually draw the answer on a diagram, or find **coordinates**.

Describe the transformation

Given an object and an image, work out what the transformation was and describe it:

- for reflection, the position of the mirror line
- for translation, the horizontal and vertical distances
- for rotation, the **angle** and direction and possibly the centre.

Solving problems with transformations

1 This reflection problem asks you to carry out a reflection and describe the result.

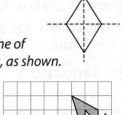

- Part of a shape is shown with its two **lines of symmetry**.
  Reflect the part shape in the lines of symmetry.
  What is the name of the complete shape?

  Reflect the starting line in the lines of symmetry, then also reflect one of the image lines to complete the symmetry. The result is a **rhombus**, *as shown.*

2 In this question, you have to analyse a transformation.

- Describe the translation from shape A to shape B shown in the diagram.

  Look at corresponding **vertices** *on the object and image (for example, the top left-hand vertex). The movement is 4 units to the left and 7 units down.*

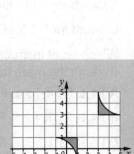

3 This rotation question does not use the centre of rotation.

- Which of these words, when rotated 180°, still makes a word?

  DID   HANNAH   MUM   EVE   NOON

  This is how the words look when rotated:

  DID   HANNAH   MUM   EVE   NOON

  NOON is the only one that still looks right.

TEST YOURSELF

1 A rectangle with vertices (1, 3), (5, 3), (5, 1) and (1, 1) is rotated 90° clockwise about the **origin**. What are the coordinates of the vertices of the image? (Draw your own diagram for this question.)

2 An object and its reflection are shown in the diagram. The end points of five lines are given. Which pair of points makes the line of reflection?

A (-1, 5) and (5, -1)

B (-5, 2) and (5, 2)

C (2, -5) and (2, 5)

D (-5, -5) and (5, 5)

E (1, 5) and (4, -4)

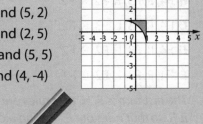

There are some types of question that don't really fit into the other topics easily. We've collected them here and called them patterns and puzzles.

It's impossible to guess exactly what the examiners will ask you to do in the test, but in this section you will find some of the most common types of 'pattern and puzzle' question.

Understanding patterns and puzzles

Some things that are common to pattern and puzzle questions are:
- links to other areas of Maths
- use of logical thinking.

*There will often be number **sequences** 'hidden' inside a question based on shape.*

Skills

Movement instructions

You have to imagine you are controlling something such as a robot and give the correct sequence of instructions to move it through a maze.

Shape sequences

The question features a shape-based pattern which grows according to a **rule**. You have to predict the number of dots, lines or shapes in the next pattern.

Fitting shapes

You need to work out how many copies of a small shape will fit inside a larger shape.

Solving pattern and puzzle problems

1 This is a maze-type question. Normally, in the test, the instructions will be written out in full: FORWARD 3, TURN RIGHT 90°, etc. We have used a code to save space:

F stands for FORWARD

R stands for TURN RIGHT 90°

L stands for TURN LEFT 90°.

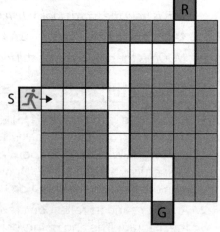

- Which set of instructions will guide the figure through the maze from square S to square G?

   A F4, L, F2, R, F3, L, F2

   B F4, R, F3, R, F2, R, F2

   C F4, R, F3, L, F3, R, F2

   D F4, R, F3, L, F2, R, F2

   E F4, R, F3, L, F2, L, F2

The first turn is R, so that rules out A. The second turn is L, so that rules out B. The third turn is R, so that rules out E, leaving a choice between C and D. The third FORWARD instruction is 2 squares, so following C would mean going through a wall! So D is the correct answer.

2 This problem contains a number sequence.

- How many white **hexagons** are needed to make the next pattern in this sequence?

   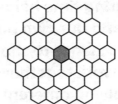

*The number of white hexagons in each pattern is **0** (+6) **6** (+12) **18** (+18) **36**.*
The difference increases by 6 each time, so the next number should be 36 + 24 = 60

3 This is a shape-fitting question.

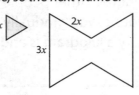

- How many of the **equilateral triangles** would you need to fill up the 'bow tie' shape?

The easiest way to tackle this problem is to draw the triangles inside the bow tie shape. 16 are required.

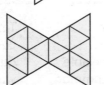

TEST YOURSELF

1 How many matchsticks are needed to make the next pattern in the sequence?

  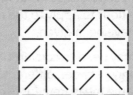

2 How many copies of the small rectangle do you need to fill up the space inside the large shape?

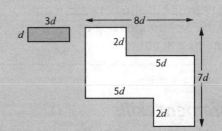

3 Which set of instructions will steer the car from the start (S) to the chequered flag (F), avoiding the oil patches?

  A F3, L, F3, R, F4, R, F4

  B F3, L, F1, R, F5, R, F3

  C F3, R, F1, L, F5, L, F1

  D F3, L, F2, R, F5, R, F4

  E F3, L, F1, R, F3, R, F2

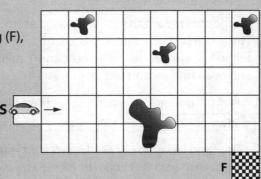

Measuring is one of the ways in which we understand the world around us. Measuring length and weight allows us to build and manufacture things. Measuring time helps us understand things as different as the seasons and our own bodies. A question on measurement gives you the chance to show that you understand how units of measurement work together and that you can undertake calculations involving different quantities.

Measurement is no use without standard units. These are lengths, weights and time intervals that everyone agrees on, so that if I say that my car journey was 50km and took me 45 minutes, other people understand what I mean. For example, when you are young, you gradually gain an understanding of how long a metre is, how heavy a kilogram is and what a minute feels like.

What to expect

In the test, you will be expected to demonstrate a number of different measurement skills. You need to be able to estimate the size or weight of common objects. In problems that have a context you need to decide what mathematical operations to apply to the measurements you have been given.

You may need to convert between units – not only between different metric units for the same measurement (e.g. millimetres and centimetres), but also between metric units and the older, imperial ones (e.g. kilograms and pounds).

Time intervals are another common source of questions – being able to work out the length of time between two events or finding out what time something will occur (e.g. what time the tumble dryer will finish if it is now 5.45pm and the drying cycle takes 100 minutes).

Some questions in the test papers may be multiple-choice. To answer them, you need to select the correct answer from the choices given. Sometimes the answer choices may be calculations involving the measurements given in the question.

Measurement skills

A solid knowledge of the units of measurement is vital to dealing with measurement questions.

1 Metric prefixes are the little 'extras' that go at the front of a unit to change its size. These can be used with any basic unit, so from the metre (m), gram (g), litre (l) and second (s) we get the millimeter (mm), milligram (mg), millilitre (ml) and even millisecond (ms).

Prefix	milli- (m)	centi- (c)	deci- (d)	deka- (da)	hecto- (h)	kilo- (k)
Effect	1000× smaller	100× smaller	10× smaller	10× bigger	100× bigger	1000× bigger

'Deci' and 'deka-' aren't used much, and you usually only hear 'hecto-' with the 'are', which is an area unit equal to 100 square metres. A hectare is an area equal to that of a square with sides 100m long, i.e. 10 000 square metres.

1 When converting between units, remember that when you are expressing a measurement using a *smaller* unit, you will need *more* of them, so you need to *multiply* by the conversion factor.

There are 100cm in 1m.   *30m = 30 × 100 = 3000cm, not 0.3cm!*

When you are expressing a measurement using a *bigger* unit, you will need *fewer* of them, so you need to *divide* by the conversion factor.

There are 1000mg in 1g.   *400mg = 400 ÷ 1000 = 0.4g, not 400 000g.*

2 Remember that time units are not decimal. Some people try to add time units by treating the minutes as hundredths of an hour, which of course they aren't. For example, suppose you needed to total up 3 hours 45 minutes and 2 hours 55 minutes. 3.45 + 2.55 = 6.00, so you might think the answer was 6 hours (this is an easy trap to fall into if you're using a calculator).

The correct answer is 5 hours (3 hours + 2 hours) and 100 minutes (45 minutes + 55 minutes), which is 6 hours and 40 minutes.

100 minutes = 1 hour and 40 minutes.

3 Estimating is a useful skill and often comes up in the context of weight. It helps to know some common objects that have certain weights as a reference for questions like these.

The weight of a bag containing 8 baking potatoes could be about 1.5kg.

A baking potato is about twice the size of an apple and an apple usually weighs about 100g, so that's 200g per potato. Multiply by 8 to get 1600 grams or 1.6kg, so the figure above is roughly right.

4 In the test, you can expect to find questions like these.

● Huw ran a marathon. He took 4 hours and 38 minutes and crossed the finishing line at 3.15pm. What time did he start running?

A 11.53am   **B** 11.23am   **C** 11.37am

D 10.23am   **E** 10.37am

Use a timeline like this one to help you.

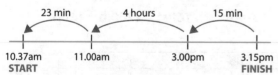

● A packet of butter weighs 250g. The packets are transported in boxes. Inside a box there are 5 layers with 24 packets in each layer. The boxes are stacked on a wooden pallet and loaded into the delivery van by forklift. The forklift can carry a maximum load of half a tonne. How many boxes can be stacked on the pallet?

There are 24 × 5 = 120 packets in a box.

These weigh $120 × 250g = 120 × \frac{1}{4}kg = 30kg$ each.

$\frac{1}{2}$ tonne = 500kg. $500 ÷ 30 = 50 ÷ 3 = 16\frac{2}{3}$.

So a maximum of 16 boxes can be stacked on the pallet.

TIPS FOR SUCCESS

Equivalents

There are two sets of equivalents you need to know:

● How the metric units are related – in other words, how many millimetres make a metre, etc.

● What the rough equivalents are for the metric and imperial units – for example, that 1 foot is almost exactly 30cm.

What you will learn

In this section you will learn about these measurement topics:

● length, capacity and weight

● time.

You use different words for different types of length. You usually talk about the length of an object but the distance between two places. Capacity is the amount of liquid a container can hold – small or large. When you talk about the weight of an object, you really mean its _mass_.

One of the difficult things about measurement is that in the UK, we use two different systems of units, the **imperial system** and the newer **metric system**. The metric system has the advantage of being completely **decimal**, but many people still use some of the old units. For example, when someone wants to know how far you live from school, do you tell them the answer in miles or kilometres?

Understanding length

The metric system of length is based on the metre.

> **1 metre (m) is divided into 100 centimetres (cm) or 1000 millimetres (mm).**
> **This also means that 10mm = 1cm and 1000m = 1 kilometre (km).**

The imperial system starts with the **inch**.

> **12 inches (in or ") = 1 foot (ft or '). 3 feet = 1 yard (yd), so 36in = 1yd.**
> **1760yd = 1 mile (mi), so 1mi = 5280ft or 63 360in.**

You need to know these rough **equivalents**.

Imperial	1in	1ft	40in	1mi	5mi
Metric	2.5cm	30cm	1m	1.6km	8km

…_when you go on a car or bus journey, you will see signs giving distances to places (in miles) or junctions (in yards), or the headroom of a bridge (in metres)._

Understanding weight

The metric system of weight (or more properly, **mass**) is based on the gram.

> **1000 grams (g) = 1 kilogram (kg). 1000kg = 1 tonne or metric ton (t).**

The imperial system starts with the **ounce**.

> **16 ounces (oz) = 1 pound (lb). 14lb = 1 stone (st). 160st = 2240lb = 1 ton.**

You need to know these rough equivalents.

Imperial	1oz	1lb	2.2lb	1st	1 ton
Metric	28g	450g	1kg	6.4kg	1t

…_if you look at a cookery book, the recipes may have the weights in both sets of units._

Understanding capacity

The metric system of **capacity** is based on the litre.

> **1000 millilitres (ml) = 1 litre (l). 10ml = 1 centilitre (cl). 100cl = 1 litre (l).**

The imperial system starts with the fluid ounce.

> **20 fluid ounces (fl oz) = 1 pint (pt). 8pt = 1 gallon (gal).**

You need to know these rough equivalents.

Imperial	1fl oz	1pt	1.75pt	1 gal
Metric	30ml	600ml	1l	4.5l

…_if you look at bottled drinks, the labels may give the capacity in both sets of units._

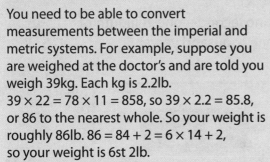

Skills

Conversions

You need to be able to convert measurements between the imperial and metric systems. For example, suppose you are weighed at the doctor's and are told you weigh 39kg. Each kg is 2.2lb.
$39 \times 22 = 78 \times 11 = 858$, so $39 \times 2.2 = 85.8$, or 86 to the nearest whole. So your weight is roughly 86lb. $86 = 84 + 2 = 6 \times 14 + 2$, so your weight is 6st 2lb.

Adjusting metric units

You may need to adjust the units at the end of a calculation so the answer is easy to understand. Suppose you had to lay railway track in 25m sections. You have 600 sections to lay. The length of the track is $600 \times 25 = 6 \times 2500 = 15\,000$m.
This isn't easy to understand, but $15\,000 \div 1000 = 15$km. Remember that when you change to a *larger* unit, you need *fewer* of them to measure the same distance, so *divide* by the conversion factor.

Reading scales

Metric scales are just like number lines, but you may see many different ways of dividing up the amounts.

Here are three examples, all showing the same weight, 2.8kg.

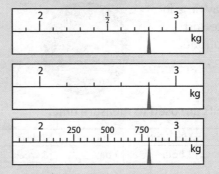

Estimating

You may be asked to make an estimate of the weight of some items. An apple weighs about 100g and a litre of water weighs 1kg. An adult typically weighs between 60 and 90kg and a 10 year old about half that.

Solving problems with length, capacity and weight

1 This problem needs an imperial to metric conversion.

- Hanif is 5 feet 4 inches tall. Which of these is closest to his height in metres?

 A 1.2m **B** 1.3m **C** 1.4m

 D 1.5m **E** 1.6m

 Change 5ft 4in to centimetres first.
 $5 \times 30 + 4 \times 2.5 = 150 + 10 = 160$cm.
 This is 1.6m, so E is the correct answer.

2 This is an estimation problem.

- Twelve adults want to use a lift. A notice inside the lift reads *MAXIMUM WEIGHT $\frac{3}{4}$ TONNE*. Should they all get in?
 $\frac{3}{4}$ *tonne is 750kg. The average adult is about 75kg and $75 \times 10 = 750$kg.*

 So the lift will only hold 10 people of average weight. They should not all get in!

TEST YOURSELF

1 Emily is weighing ingredients for a cake. The scale currently shows this weight.

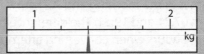

She needs to add 800g dried fruit to the mixture. What will the scale read after she adds it?

 A 1.48kg **B** 1.804kg **C** 2kg

 D 2.2kg **E** 2.4kg

2 Carlo's baby sister drinks 600ml of milk each day. How many litres of milk does she drink in a week?

3 On holiday in France, Josh sees a road sign saying PARIS 320km. How far is this distance in miles?

Time

Time is a vital part of our lives. We use the language of time constantly, whenever we say how long something took, or how long it will take, or when something will start or finish.

Units of time range from the very short (a nanosecond – one-billionth of a second) to the very long (a millennium – one thousand years).

Understanding time

We display time in **analogue** and **digital** formats.

analogue

digital

These units are used to measure time.

60 seconds	60 minutes	24 hours	7 days	28–31 days	365–366 days
1 minute	1 hour	1 day	1 week	1 month	1 year

To remember how many days there are in each month, use the old rhyme:

'Thirty days have September, April, June and November; all the rest have thirty-one, excepting February alone, which has twenty-eight days clear, and twenty-nine in each leap year.'

The extra day in February is the reason why a leap year, which occurs every four years, has 366 days.

Time skills

Using the 12-hour and 24-hour clock

12-hour times use am and pm to distinguish between morning and the rest of the day, so 7.21am is in the morning and 7.21pm is in the evening. In 24-hour time, these would be written 07:21 and 19:21. The difference between these times is 12 hours, so add or subtract 12 from the hours when converting afternoon and evening times from one system to the other.

	morning	noon	afternoon/evening	midnight
12-hour time	12.01am – 11.59am	12.00 noon	12.01pm – 11.59pm	12.00 midnight
24-hour time	00.01 – 11.59	12.00	12.01 – 23.59	00.00 *(not 24.00)*

Time intervals

You may be asked to work out the difference between two times – this is called a time interval. A rough timeline can be useful.

For example, if you need to know how long it is from 4.25pm until 7.10pm, you can set it out this way:

The total is 2 hours 45 minutes.

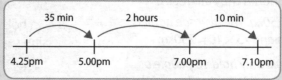

Multiplying and dividing times

If you have to multiply or divide a length of time, you may have to change units. For example, if a factory can make a Widget every 25 minutes, how long will it take to make 50 Widgets?

$50 \times 25 = 1250$ minutes. $1250 \div 60 = 20$, with **remainder** 50.

So the time taken is 20 hours 50 minutes.

Your day

What fraction of a day do you spend doing various things? Work out how long you spend sleeping, how long you are at school, etc. as a fraction of 24 hours.

You could even make a **pie chart** of your day. How many degrees would represent 1 hour?

Solving problems with time

1   This problem asks for the **range** of a set of times.
Calculating this is the same as finding a time interval.

- Mandy kept a record of how long she spent on her computer in one week.
What is the range of her times?

Day	Mon	Tue	Wed	Thu	Fri	Sat	Sun
Time spent	1hr 20min	1hr 35min	25min	1hr 45min	2hr 15min	3hr 5min	2hr 10min

The range is the difference between the maximum and minimum.

This is 3hr 5min – 25min.

You can think of this as 2hr 65min – 25min = 2hr 40min.

2   This is a division problem that requires a change of units.

- Harry's parents paid for 10 hours of piano lessons.
The lessons are 40 minutes long.
How many lessons have they paid for?

10 hours = 10 × 60 = 600 minutes

600 ÷ 40 = 60 ÷ 4 = 15 lessons

3   In this question you need to express one time as a **fraction** of another.

- What fraction of 3 minutes is 2 minutes 30 seconds?

3 minutes = 180 seconds and 2 minutes 30 seconds = 150 seconds

The fraction is $\frac{150}{180} = \frac{15}{18} = \frac{5}{6}$.

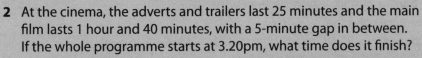

1   How should the time 4.45 in the afternoon be written?

A 14:45   **B** 16:45   **C** 18:45   **D** 04:45   **E** 15:45

2   At the cinema, the adverts and trailers last 25 minutes and the main film lasts 1 hour and 40 minutes, with a 5-minute gap in between. If the whole programme starts at 3.20pm, what time does it finish?

3   At the swimming pool where Simone swims, you pay £3 per hour to use the pool. Simone goes to twelve 40-minute sessions in a month. How much does this cost?

Glossary

2-D shape	a shape that has only two dimensions, such as length and width, but no thickness, e.g. a square
3-D shape	a shape that has three dimensions: height, width and depth, e.g. a cube. 3-D shapes are sometimes called solid shapes
acute angle	an angle less than 90°
adjacent angle	adjacent angles are two angles on a straight line that are next to each other and meet at the same point. Adjacent angles add up to 180°
algebra	the branch of Maths in which letters are used instead of numbers, e.g. $6 + b = 8$. You can use algebra to find missing numbers or you can use it to write down a rule connecting different numbers
analogue clock	a 12-hour clock face that has two rotating hands to show the hours and minutes, and sometimes a third to show the seconds
angle	a measure of turn between two lines meeting at the same point. Angles are measured in degrees (°)
anticlockwise	turning in this direction ↺
arc	a section of the outside of a circle
area	a measure of the amount of space a 2-D shape takes up. Area is measured in square units, e.g. cm^2, m^2, km^2
ascending order	where numbers are arranged from smallest to largest
axis (plural axes)	the horizontal and vertical lines on a graph which join or intersect (cross). The horizontal axis is called the x-axis and the vertical axis is called the y-axis
BIDMAS	the order in which we do mathematical operations: brackets, indices (powers), division and multiplication, addition and subtraction
capacity	a measure of the amount of liquid a container can hold. Capacity is measured in millilitres (ml), litres (l), etc.
circumference	the distance around the outside of a circle
clockwise	turning in this direction ↻
common denominator	when two or more fractions have the same denominator, e.g. $\frac{2}{6}$ and $\frac{5}{6}$ have a common denominator
common factor	a factor that is common to two or more numbers, e.g. the factors of 6 are 1, 2, 3 and 6; the factors of 9 are 1, 3 and 9, so the common factors are 1 and 3
common multiple	a multiple that is common to two or more numbers, e.g. 24 is a common multiple of 8 and 6 ($3 \times 8 = 24$ and $4 \times 6 = 24$)
compound shape	when two or more shapes are joined together to make another shape
concave polygon	a polygon with at least one reflex angle
consecutive number	numbers that follow each other when counting, e.g. 101, 102 and 103 are consecutive
conversion graph	a straight line graph used to convert one unit into another, e.g. ounces into grams
coordinates	a set of values that show an exact position on a grid, e.g. (3, 5) is 3 units across and 5 units up
cube	a 3-D shape that has 6 identical square faces, 8 vertices (corners) and 12 equal edges
cube number	the result of multiplying a number by itself twice, e.g. to calculate the cube of 2 (2^3) you do $2 \times 2 \times 2 = 8$
cuboid	a 3-D shape with six rectangular faces
decagon	a ten-sided polygon
decimal	decimals are the digits (numbers) to the right of the decimal point, e.g. tenths, hundredths, thousandths, etc.
decimal place value system	a number system based on 10. Each place holds digits that are ten times larger or smaller than the next place, e.g. 0.2, 2, 20

denominator	the number on the bottom of the fraction, e.g. in $\frac{2}{3}$, 3 is the denominator. It shows how many parts the whole has been divided into
descending order	where numbers are arranged from largest to smallest
diameter	the distance straight across a circle from one point on the outside to the opposite point, passing through the centre
digital clock	a clock that uses numbers instead of hands to show the time
equation	a mathematical statement which always includes an equals sign and says that two things are the same. An algebraic equation uses letters or symbols instead of numbers, e.g. $x + 3 = 7$ (if $x + 3$ is equal to 7, x must be 4)
equilateral triangle	a triangle where all sides and angles are equal
equivalent	having the same value or amount
equivalent fraction	fractions that have the same value, e.g. $\frac{1}{2}$ and $\frac{2}{4}$ are equivalent fractions
equivalent ratio	ratios that have the same value, e.g. 6 : 8 and 3 : 4 are equivalent ratios
expression	in algebra, a group of terms added or subtracted, e.g. $2a + 3b - c$
factor	a number that divides exactly into another number, e.g. 3 and 5 divide exactly into 15 and so are factors of 15
formula (plural formulae)	a formula uses letters or words to give a rule
fraction	a part of a whole. It is expressed in the form $\frac{1}{2}$
frequency	the number of times something appears in a given set of data, or occurs in a given time period
heptagon	a seven-sided polygon
hexagon	a six-sided polygon
highest common factor (HCF)	the highest factor that is common to two or more numbers, e.g. the highest common factor of 12 and 8 is 4
horizontal	a horizontal line is a straight level line across
image	the resulting shape after applying a transformation to an object shape
imperial system	a system of weights and measures used in the UK before we adopted the metric system. Imperial measures include ounces, pounds and stones and inches, feet and miles
improper fraction	in an improper fraction, the numerator is greater than the denominator e.g. $\frac{7}{4}$
index (plural indices)	this tells us how many times the base number (large number in a power) is multiplied by itself. It is the small number to the right of the base, e.g. in 3^2, 2 is the index number
integer	a whole number that can be positive or negative, including zero
interior angle	the angle formed inside a polygon by two sides that meet at a point
inverse	an inverse is a mathematical opposite. Subtraction is the inverse of addition and division is the inverse of multiplication
isosceles triangle	a triangle with two equal sides and two equal angles
kite	a quadrilateral with two pairs of equal sides and one line of symmetry
like terms	terms whose variables (letters/symbols that represent numbers) are the same, e.g. in the expression $2b + 3c + 5b$, $2b$ and $5b$ are like terms because they both have the variable b
line of symmetry	the 'mirror line' that turns an object into its reflection

Glossary

lowest (or least) common denominator (LCD)	also termed the least common denominator, the smallest number that the denominators of two or more fractions will divide into exactly, e.g. the LCD of $\frac{4}{5}$ and $\frac{5}{10}$ is 20 ($20 \div 5 = 4$ and $20 \div 10 = 2$)
lowest (or least) common multiple (LCM)	also termed the least common multiple, the smallest number that is a common multiple of two or more numbers, e.g. the lowest common multiple of 3 and 4 is 12 ($3 \times 4 = 12$)
lowest terms	when a fraction or ratio has been simplified as far as possible, also called the 'simplest form', e.g. $\frac{3}{4}$ is $\frac{9}{12}$ given in its lowest terms
mass	the measurement we usually call 'weight' is more properly called mass. Mass is measured in milligrams (mg), grams (g), kilograms (kg), etc.
mean	a measure of average. To calculate the mean you add all the numbers together and divide by how many numbers there are
median	a measure of average. It is the middle value of an ordered set of numbers
metric system	the decimal system for measuring lengths – it uses multiples of 10. Metric measures include kilometres (km), millilitres (ml), grams (g), etc.
mirror line	the line of reflection
mixed number	a whole number and a fraction together e.g. $3\frac{1}{4}$
mode	a measure of average. It is the object or quantity that occurs the most. It is possible to have more than one mode or no mode at all
multiple	the result of multiplying one integer by other integers, e.g. the first five multiples of 5 are 5, 10, 15, 20 and 25
negative number	a number less than zero
net	a flat shape that can be folded to make a 3-D shape
nonagon	a nine-sided polygon
number bonds	pairs of whole numbers that combine together to a give a particular total
numerator	the number on the top of a fraction, e.g. in $\frac{2}{3}$, 2 is the numerator. It represents the number of parts of the whole
object	the original shape before a transformation has been applied
obtuse angle	an angle greater than 90° but less than 180°
octagon	an eight-sided polygon
operation	addition, subtraction, multiplication and division are operations
origin	where the x-axis and the y-axis cross. The coordinate point (0, 0)
outcome	one of the possible results from a probability experiment
parallel	parallel lines never meet and are always set at the same distance apart
parallelogram	a quadrilateral with two pairs of parallel sides
pentagon	a five-sided polygon
percentage	the number of parts per hundred, e.g. 20% is 20 parts out of 100
perimeter	the distance around the outside of a shape
perpendicular	when two lines cross or meet at right-angles
pie chart	a circular chart where each section of the 'pie' represents a part or fraction of the total
polygon	a flat shape that has three or more straight sides
positive number	a number greater than zero
prime number	a number that has exactly two factors, 1 and itself
prism	a 3-D shape that has two identical ends, e.g. cylinder
probability	the chance or possibility that something will happen
proportion	quantities are in proportion to each other if their ratios stay the same as the quantities get larger or smaller

pyramid	a solid shape with sides that meet in a point and a base that is flat, e.g. cone, square-based pyramid, etc.
quadrant	any one of the four regions on a coordinate graph
quadrilateral	a 2-D shape with four sides, e.g. square, rhombus, trapezium, kite, etc.
radius	the distance from the centre to the outside of a circle
range	the difference between the highest and lowest values of a set of data
ratio	ratios are used to compare two or more numbers or quantities. Things that are proportional to each other always stay in a fixed ratio, e.g. the ratio legs : cows is 4 : 1
reflection	the image of a shape as it would be seen in a mirror
reflective symmetry	a shape has reflective symmetry if one half is the mirror image of the other
reflex angle	an angle greater than 180°
regular polygon	a polygon where all sides and angles are equal
remainder	the number left over when one number doesn't divide exactly into another
rhombus	a quadrilateral with sides of equal length
right angle	an angle of 90°
rotation	to turn an object about a given point
rotational symmetry	a shape has rotational symmetry if it looks the same after being rotated by less than a full turn. The order of rotational symmetry is the number of different angles up to 360° that a shape can be turned through and look the same, e.g. order 4 would be 90°, 180°, 270°, 360°
rule	rules usually tell you what you need to do to a number in a sequence to get to the next number
scalene triangle	a triangle in which all the sides and all the angles are different
sequence	a list or pattern of numbers that are usually set out in an order, e.g. 2, 4, 6, 8…
simplest form	see lowest terms
simplify	to collect together like terms to make algebraic expressions less complicated
solid shape	see 3-D shape
sphere	a 3-D shape that is perfectly round
square number	the result of multiplying a number by itself, e.g. 4 is the square of 2 ($2 \times 2 = 4$)
square root	finding the square root is the inverse (opposite) of squaring, e.g. the square root of 4 is 2 ($2 \times 2 = 4$)
surface area	the total area of all the faces on a solid shape
term	a part of an expression, e.g. in the expression $2a + 3b$, $2a$ is the first term; a part of a sequence, e.g. in 2, 4, 6, 8… the first term is 2
transformation	an action that changes the size or position of a shape
translation	moving a shape to a different place without reflecting or rotating it
trapezium	a four-sided shape that has one pair of parallel sides
triangular number	numbers which, if you arranged as a pattern of dots, would make a triangle, e.g. 3, 6 and 10 are triangular numbers
unit fraction	a fraction with a numerator of 1
vertex (plural vertices)	a point where lines meet, a corner
vertical	a vertical line is a line that goes straight up or down
volume	the amount of 3-D space filled by an object. It is measured in cubic units, e.g. cm^3, m^3, etc.

The next steps

Now you have completed your practice, you are ready to take the second set of more challenging Practice tests.

These Practice tests (located in the pull-out booklet) will confirm your ability to answer harder questions and highlight any areas that still need extra work.

Taking the second tests

Follow the guidance on page 10 for timing, equipment, surroundings, question types and tips then take the following tests in the order as outlined below.

Maths test 2: 45 minutes

Mental maths test 2: about 15 minutes.

Remember: this is a test to help you to find your strengths and weaknesses. Because of this it is important not to choose a multiple-choice option or guess randomly if you don't know the answer. In these instances it is better to leave the answer line blank.

Marking

Once you have completed the tests you will be ready to mark them. The process to follow is simple – the stages are listed below.

Maths test 2

- Turn to *Maths* grid 2 on page 81 and complete it, following the instructions on page 11.
- Transfer the total number of marks to the Summary box on page 83 and work out the percentage as directed.

Mental maths test 2

- Turn to *Mental maths grid 2* on page 82 and complete it, following the instructions on page 11.
- Transfer the total number of marks to the Summary box on page 83 and work out the percentage as directed.

Mental maths grid 2

Follow the instructions on page 11 to fill in this grid and page 13 for

	Question	Mark*	Skill
Numbers and their properties	1		Ordering and rounding whole numbers
	2		Number patterns and sequences
	3		Factors and multiples
Calculations	4		Adding and subtracting whole numbers
	5		
	6		Multiplying and dividing whole numbers
	7		
	8		Solving problems involving the four operations
Fractions, decimals and percentages	9		Algebra
	10		Fractions
	11		Fraction calculations
	12		Decimals
	13		Finding equivalents
	14		Percentage calculations
	15		Ratio and proportion
Working with charts and data	16		Finding the mode, median, mean and range
	17		Probability
Shape and space	18		2-D and 3-D shapes
	19		Angles
	20		
Measuring	21		Perimeter, area and volume
	22		
	23		Length, capacity and weight
	24		
	25		Time

*1 mark is allocated for each correct answer. There are no half marks.

Total [/25] Add up your total for your Menta

82

80

Follow the instructions on page 11 to fill in this grid and page 13 for instructions for use.

Numbers and their properties

Question	Mark*	Skill	Page	To do	Try it out	Test yourself
1		Ordering and rounding whole numbers	18			
2						
3						
4		Number patterns and sequences	20			
5						
6		Factors and multiples	22			
7						
Total	/7	Read 'Introducing numbers and their properties' first on pages 16–17 if you have missed any Skills in the Numbers and their properties section.				

Calculations

Question	Mark*	Skill	Page	To do	Try it out	Test yourself
8		Adding and subtracting whole numbers	26			
9						
10						
11		Multiplying and dividing whole numbers	28			
12						
13						
14		Solving problems involving the four operations	30			
15						
16		Algebra	32			
17						
Total	/10	Read 'Introducing calculations' first on pages 24–25 if you have missed any Skills in the Calculations section.				

Fractions, decimals and percentages

Question	Mark*	Skill	Page	To do	Try it out	Test yourself
18		Fractions	36			
19		Fraction calculations	38			
20						
21		Decimals	40			
22						
23		Finding equivalents	42			
24						
25		Percentage calculations	44			
26						
27		Ratio and proportion	46			
28						
Total	/11	Read 'Introducing fractions, decimals and percentages' first on pages 34–35 if you have missed any Skills in the Fractions, decimals and percentages section.				

Working with charts and data

Question	Mark*	Skill	Page	To do	Try it out	Test yourself
29		Charts and graphs	50			
30						
31		Finding the mode, median, mean and range	52			
32						
33		Probabilty	54			
34						
Total	/6	Read 'Introducing working with charts and data' first on pages 48–49 if you have missed any Skills in the Working with charts and data section.				

Maths grid 2

Shape and space

Question	Mark*	Skill	Page	To do	Try it out	Test yourself
35		2-D and 3-D shapes	58			
36						
37		Angles	60			
38						
39		Perimeter, area and volume	62			
40						
41		Coordinates	64			
42						
43		Reflection, translation and rotation	66			
44						
45		Patterns and puzzles	68			
46						
Total	/12	Read 'Introducing shape and space' first on pages 56-57 if you have missed any Skills in the Shape and space section.				

Measuring

Question	Mark*	Skill	Page	To do	Try it out	Test yourself
47		Length, capacity and weight	72			
48						
49		Time	74			
50						
Total	/4	Read 'Introducing measuring' first on pages 70–71 if you have missed any Skills in the Measuring section.				

*1 mark is allocated for each correct answer. There are no half marks.

Total [/50] **Add up your total for your Maths test here.**

Mental maths grid 2

Follow the instructions on page 11 to fill in this grid and page 13 for instructions for use.

	Question	Mark*	Skill	Page	To do
Numbers and their properties	1		Ordering and rounding whole numbers	18	
	2		Number patterns and sequences	20	
	3		Factors and multiples	22	
Calculations	4		Adding and subtracting whole numbers	26	
	5				
	6		Multiplying and dividing whole numbers	28	
	7				
	8		Solving problems involving the four operations	30	
	9		Algebra	32	
Fractions, decimals and percentages	10		Fractions	36	
	11		Fraction calculations	38	
	12		Decimals	40	
	13		Finding equivalents	42	
	14		Percentage calculations	44	
	15		Ratio and proportion	46	
Working with charts and data	16		Finding the mode, median, mean and range	52	
	17		Probabilty	54	
Shape and space	18		2-D and 3-D shapes	58	
	19		Angles	60	
	20		Perimeter, area and volume	62	
	21				
Measuring	22		Length, capacity and weight	72	
	23				
	24				
	25		Time	74	

*1 mark is allocated for each correct answer. There are no half marks.

Total [/25] **Add up your total for your Mental maths test here.**

Now that you have all your results from the second set of Practice tests you can celebrate your success in areas where you have improved and plan for your final preparations.

Reviewing the final summary boxes

Look at your results in the Summary boxes below and review your scores. To be prepared for the 11+ tests you should be aiming to achieve results of 80% or higher.

If you still have areas that need additional practice you can…

- revisit the relevant pages in the guide
- purchase additional materials linked to the specific skills you have identified in these tests.

If you are now achieving the suggested percentages, you should move on to take some 11+ practice tests to boost your confidence and further develop your familiarity with the different question types you may encounter. These tests are also useful for increasing your speed in answering the questions.

Practice support

You may find the following Letts titles helpful for additional skills practice…

- Maths Ages 9–10 Assessment Papers Levels 3–5   9781844192243
- Maths Ages 10–11 Assessment Papers Levels 3–5   9781844192250
- More Maths Ages 10–11 Years Assessment Papers Levels 3–5   9781844195541

You may find the following Letts Practice papers helpful for your final preparations…

- 11+ Practice Papers Standard Maths   9781844192434
- 11+ Practice Papers Multiple Choice Maths   9781844192502

Summary boxes

Maths test 2

Total

Percentage

Work out your percentage using this sum

$\frac{\text{Total}}{50} \times 100 =$

Mental maths test 2

Total

Percentage

Work out your percentage using this sum

$\frac{\text{Total}}{25} \times 100 =$

Cover up

Work out how many pound coins you would you need to cover your bedroom floor…

- Measure the diameter of your pound coin.
- Measure the length and width of your bedroom.
- Work out how many rows of coins you would need to cover the floor completely using this information.

Check your answer with a calculator to work out the 'price' of your bedroom!

The daisy challenge

Petal picking

Pick ten daisies. Carefully count the number of petals on each daisy and keep a record of how many there are on each.

With this data, work out…

- the mean number of petals
- the mode number of petals
- the median
- the range.

The longest daisy chain

Take this 'daisy challenge' with a friend.

You each have 15 minutes to see who can make the longest daisy chain. Time yourselves. Measure your chains in metres and centimetres to find the winner.

Can you convert these lengths into yards, feet and inches?

Fruity mixes

Test your ratio and proportion skills as you try to make the perfect tropical fruit cocktail.

You will need: a small medicine measure, four glasses, a carton of orange juice, a carton of pineapple juice, a bottle of lemonade.

Mix the orange juice, lemonade and pineapple juice in the proportions shown in the table, using the medicine measure.

Ask your family to vote for their favourite 'cocktail' mix.

Name your special cocktail and mix one for everyone in the same proportions!

Juice	Glass 1	Glass 2	Glass 3	Glass 4
	Number of medicine measures			
Orange	1	2	3	2
Lemonade	2	3	2	2
Pineapple	3	1	1	2

Football forecast

Find a football league table in the paper or on the Internet.

Write down the table, listing…

- the top 10 teams
- their points total for the season so far.

Use the system of 2 points for a win and 1 point for a draw and work out which teams could win the league if it finishes in 10 weeks' time.

Animal addition

Practise your adding skills on a car journey with this animal addition game. Decide which of the following you are going to count before you set off…

- eyes (counting in 2s)
- legs (counting in 4s)

Every time you see an animal you must count the eyes or the legs and add them to your total. The game gets more interesting when you see a field of cows or sheep!

TRY IT OUT

Number magic

Surprise a friend with this number game.

Ask them to think of a number between 1 and 10 (and not to tell you what the number is). Now ask them to do the following calculation in their head, one step at a time…

- Multiply by 3.
- Add 4. Take away 1.
- Take away 3.
- Divide by 3.

Now they will be back to their original number. Tell them that you guess their answer is the number they began with.

Now make up your own calculations, making sure the calculations balance.

Countdown to the tests

As soon as possible before the tests...

Check with the school you are applying to about their entrance requirements:

- Find out what exams your chosen school will be setting.
- Make sure you know the dates.

One week before the tests

- Check your travel arrangements and practise getting to the destination to make sure you know where to go.
- Make sure you have enough pens, pencils and an analogue watch so you can see how much time you have spent if you are timing your work.
- Check with the school if you need geometry equipment (ruler, set squares, protractor, compasses) and whether you can bring tracing paper and a mirror. Any equipment will need to be taken in a see-through pencil case.

During the week before the tests

- Allow yourself 90 minutes to check through any areas you're worried about up to two days before.
- Avoid last minute practice as this can make you anxious – do something with your friends or parents to help you relax the night before.
- Get a good night's sleep.

The day of the tests

- Eat a good breakfast.
- Leave in plenty of time, making allowances for traffic and other hold-ups.
- Take a healthy snack to boost your energy levels and a small bottle of water.
- Go to the toilet before you go in to the test.

During the tests

- Read the questions twice before you start writing.
- Make sure you understand what you are expected to do. For example, make sure you know how many selections you are being asked to make in multiple-choice questions and how you are supposed to mark down your answer.
- Underline key words in the questions.
- Make sure you know which questions get most marks. Spend your time accordingly.
- After half the time is up, check whether you have got to the stapled pages in the test. If you haven't, go through and do the easy questions in the second half of the paper.
- Even if you are in a hurry, make sure your work is easy to read.
- If you can't do a question, leave it. Come back to it at the end if you have time.
- Leave time at the end to check your work.

Maths papers

- Look through the paper and think about answering the questions to which you know the answers first.
- If you are provided, or allowed to bring, mirrors and tracing paper, use them to help you answer questions more easily.
- Remember, if you are not provided with spare paper you should be able to jot your working on the test paper.

Many schools base their final selection on how well the applicants perform in an interview.

With the right preparation, you can use this opportunity to show your potential to be a good member of the school and find out whether this is the right place for you.

Discussion topics

Being prepared with interesting things to talk about during your interview is always a good idea.

If you have recently visited a museum, National Trust or English Heritage property these make ideal subjects to prepare for discussion. If you have taken part in a sporting event such as a rugby tournament or a cross-country run, these make equally good talking points.

Rather than writing down lots of information, take a small business card and create a spider diagram on the back. This diagram will remind you of the key points of interest that you can talk about, given the right opportunity by the interviewer.

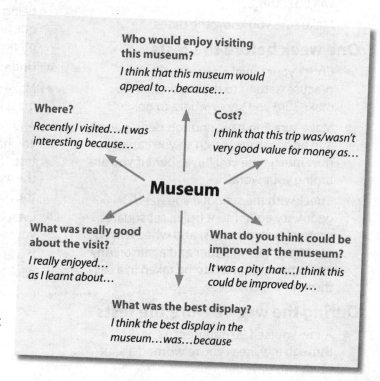

Who would enjoy visiting this museum?
I think that this museum would appeal to…because…

Where?
Recently I visited…It was interesting because…

Cost?
I think that this trip was/wasn't very good value for money as…

Museum

What was really good about the visit?
I really enjoyed… as I learnt about…

What do you think could be improved at the museum?
It was a pity that…I think this could be improved by…

What was the best display?
I think the best display in the museum…was…because

Meeting the interviewer

Waiting

- Calm yourself with the breathing techniques shown in the box, opposite.
- Do talk to other candidates who are waiting, but don't pester them for information.
- Read useful information on posters and notice boards in the room.

Entering the interview room

- Knock before you enter.
- Say 'hello' in a friendly and polite way.
- Shake hands firmly if the interviewer offers their hand.
- Wait for the interviewer to indicate a seat before you sit down.

RELAX

These techniques can help to calm your nerves when you are waiting to go into the interview room.

- Imagine you are holding an eggshell in each hand. This helps to relax your fingers and release tension.
- Breathe in slowly through your nose, counting to three and breathe out at the same pace. Concentrate on your breathing to clear your mind.

Body language

Basic body language

- Sit in a relaxed way, but don't slouch.
- Sit so that your body, including your legs and feet, points towards the interviewer.
- Don't put up barriers by crossing your arms in front of you.
- Smile, but only when appropriate – don't just grin all the time.

Hands

- Keep your hands away from your face and hair.
- Don't touch your nose before you answer a question.
- Use your hands to express yourself, but keep them on your lap at other times.

Eye contact

- Look at the interviewer, but don't stare – remember to blink.
- Don't be tempted to look away if they ask a difficult question.
- Don't shut your eyes while you think about a question.

Asking and answering questions

Avoiding yes/no answers

- Every question is an opportunity to tell the interviewer something about yourself.
- Don't just answer 'Yes' or 'No'. Give *positive* answers.

DRESS

First impressions are important. Find out in advance about what you should wear. Your current school uniform is usually a suitable option.

- Make sure that the clothes you are wearing are clean and ironed and that your shoes are clean.
- Make sure your hair is tidy and that your fringe isn't too long so that your eyes can be seen. If your hair is long, tie it back.

- Try adding an example to your answer, or qualify it ('No, but …', 'Yes, although I sometimes …').

Difficult questions

- If you're asked about an area of weakness, explain how you've tried to improve.
- If you're asked a factual question and don't know the answer, say so.
- If you don't understand a question, ask for it to be repeated or ask for an explanation.

Asking questions

- Prepare your own questions in advance.
- Don't ask questions you could easily find out the answers to.
- Ask a question that shows you have done some research about the school and would like to find out more.

Ending the interview

Thanking the interviewer

- Thank the interviewer for their time.
- Add something like, 'I've enjoyed talking with you.'

Saying goodbye

- Respond with a firm handshake if the interviewer offers their hand.
- Close the door quietly when you leave.

QUESTIONS

Think about questions you could ask at the end of your interview. They could be questions about the school in general or about specific subjects or sports that interest you. Here are some examples:

- What is special about your secondary school that is different from the other schools in the area?
- What are the most popular universities students choose when leaving the school?
- I really enjoy rugby. Are there opportunities to take part in inter-school competitions?

Once you have taken the tests, the marking and admissions process begins.

Although you'll need to wait to hear if you have been given a place at the school, you can spend some of the time finding out about what happens next.

Waiting for results

Results for the 11+ tests do not come quickly and you should expect to wait between 10 and 16 weeks. If the school you have applied to has not already told you when the results will be available, ask a parent to check the date with the school or the Local Education Authority (LEA).

Understanding the results

The pass mark

The pass mark can change from year to year as it is based on how many places there are at the school. You may also find that the pass mark for boys and girls is different – this happens when a school wants to balance the number of students from each sex in the year group.

Standardisation

In order to make the testing process fair, scores are *standardised* by age. This means that if you are one of the younger children in your age group, the school will take this into account when deciding your final marks.

When the results are not as you expect

Offers from LEA schools

If you have applied to an LEA school, you will have been offered a choice of up to three schools.

If you don't get into your first choice of school, your name will be placed on the list for your second choice. Although the schools generally take students who have put them down first on the list, there are sometimes a few spare places. If your second choice of school is full then you will be passed on to your third choice, so don't give up hope!

Offers from private and independent schools

If you have applied to a private or independent school you will not be offered an alternative school unless you have applied to these separately and taken their 11+ tests as well.

What to do if you don't agree with the result

If you haven't been lucky enough to get a place at your chosen school, your family have a right to find out why. It may be that your test results were the reason for being turned down but there could also be other reasons such as the distance you live from the school.

When you have found out the reasons but you're not happy with what you have been told, your family can put in an 'appeal' (if it is a local authority school) to see if you can get the decision changed.

Although appeals are usually carried out in a friendly way, the process is quite formal. There are a number of organisations that can help with advice, including the Advisory Centre for Education (ACE). There is also a wide selection of private companies who specialise in supporting families in putting appeals forward.

Ordering and rounding whole numbers 18

1 **a** £224 950   **b** £225 000   **c** £200 000

2 **E**: Newcastle

Number patterns and sequences 20

1 All the numbers are either triangular or prime, but only 3 is both, so the answer is 3.

2 $9 = (5 \times 2) - 1$, $17 = (9 \times 2) - 1$, etc. So the next number is $(129 \times 2) - 1 = 257$.

3 **B**: rows A and D don't have a square in the first column, so it's B, C or E. E doesn't have a prime in the second column, so it's B or C. It's row B.

Factors and multiples 22

1 **E**: 14, 13, 9 and 11 are not multiples of 4 or 5.

2 The factors of 36 are 1, 2, 3, 4, 6, 9, 12, 18, 36. Of these, 1, 4, 9 and 36 are square, so the answer is 4.

3 The multiples of 45 are 45, 90, 135, 180, 225, 270, 315, 360, 405, 450… The first one of these that is a multiple of 50 is 450, so the answer is that 450 seconds will pass.

Adding and subtracting whole numbers 26

1 $45 + 40 + 61 = 45 + 101 = 146$;
   $180 - 146 = 34$

2 $67 + 49 = 66 + 50 = 116$; $200 - 116 = 84$

Multiplying and dividing whole numbers 28

1 $308 \div 7 = 44$ weeks.

2 $252 \times 12 = 3024$ cans.

3 $5 \times 5 \times 5 \times 5 = 625$ $\sqrt{625} = 25$

Solving problems involving the four operations 30

1 $(76 - 48) \div (12 \div 3) = 28 \div 4 = 7$

2 **C**: Jared scored 310 $((8 \times 20) + (3 \times 50))$, 200, 100, 210 and 340. Mean = $1160 \div 5 = 232$

   Callum scored 300, 280, 150, 140 and 300. Mean = $1170 \div 5 = 234$

   The difference was 2 points per level.

Algebra 32

1 $x = 1\frac{1}{2}$

   subtract 4 from both sides: $6x = 2x + 6$

   subtract $2x$ from both sides: $4x = 6$

   divide both sides by 4: $x = 1.5$

2 **A**: Joyti's brother is now $y + 2$ years old. In 5 years time, he will be $y + 2 + 5$, so the correct answer is $y + 7$

Fractions 36

1 The lowest common denominator is 20. The fractions are equivalent to $\frac{11}{20}, \frac{16}{20}, \frac{10}{20}, \frac{15}{20}, \frac{14}{20}$, so the order is $\frac{1}{2}, \frac{11}{20}, \frac{7}{10}, \frac{3}{4}, \frac{4}{5}$,

   that is C, A, E, D, B.

2 **B** and **D**: $\frac{2}{8} = \frac{1}{4}$, so $\frac{2}{8}$ and $\frac{3}{4}$ add up to 1.

3 $4\frac{3}{8} = \frac{32}{8} + \frac{3}{8} = \frac{35}{8}$

Fraction calculations 38

1 There are nine numbers in the list. Of these, 6 (3, 5, 7, 11, 13, 17) are prime. Remember that 1 is not prime. So the fraction is $\frac{6}{9} = \frac{2}{3}$.

2 $\frac{3}{10}$ is left, so she must have spent $\frac{7}{10}$ of her money.
   $\frac{1}{10}$ must be £56 ÷ 7 = £8,
   so originally she had £8 × 10 = £80,
   so she has £80 − £56 = £24 left.

3 What is left in the bag is $\frac{1}{3}$ of what was there before Zoltan ate some, so that must have been 6 sweets. That is $\frac{1}{3}$ of the number in the bag before Joanna ate hers, which must have been 18. Finally, that is $\frac{1}{3}$ of what was in the bag to start with, so that must have been 54 sweets.

Decimals 40

1 Rounding to the nearest penny, with money, means 2 decimal places, so the answer is £16.29

2 **B**: the easiest way to solve this problem is to change to pence first: 2550p ÷ 30 = 85p

   Or you could work it out like this:

   $255 \div 3 = 85$, so $25.5 \div 3 = 8.5$
   and $25.5 \div 30 = 0.85$

   so each fish cost 85p

3 Each division is 0.2 so the arrow must point to 1.8

Finding equivalents 42

1 **A**: written as decimals, they are 0.018, 0.18, about $\frac{1}{20} = 0.05$, 0.081, 0.108, so 1.8% is the smallest.

2 **A**: the differences from 1 are 0.01, 0.05, 0.05, 0.03, 0.02, so 0.99 is closest.

3 **C**: they are all equal to $\frac{1}{5}$ except for C, 2%, which is $\frac{1}{50}$.

4 $\frac{21}{28}$ is shaded. This is equivalent to $\frac{3}{4}$, which is 75%.

Percentage calculations 44

1 To solve this problem, it is easiest to first find out how many tickets won. You need to divide 500 by 100 to find 1% so 1% = 5 tickets. 1% × 4 = 4%, so you need to multiply 5 tickets (1%) by 4 to find 4% of the tickets: 5 tickets × 4 = 20 tickets. 20 tickets won a prize so the answer is that 480 tickets didn't win.

2 **D**: they are all equal to £25, except D, 30% of £75, which is £22.50

3 20% is $\frac{1}{5}$. $\frac{1}{5}$ of 120 pence = 24 pence (120 ÷ 5). Adding this to the original price gives the answer £1.44

Improve your skills answers

Ratio and proportion 46

1 **C**: they are all equivalent to 4 : 3, except C, 24 : 16 = 3 : 2

2 3 shares = 18 children, so 1 share = 6. There are 8 shares altogether, so there are 48 children in the choir.

3 The real plane is 72 × 20cm = 1440cm, or 14.4m.

4 The percentage is proportional to the number of jars. 15% is equal to 45 jars, so 1% = 3 jars. The percentage for strawberry is 55%, so this is 165 jars.

Charts and graphs 50

1 Music has 2 'tens' and one 'less than 10', so the answer is between 20 and 29.

2 **E**: reading up from 1.5 on the kilograms axis to the graph line and then across to the pounds axis gives the answer 3.3 pounds.

Finding the mode, median, mean and range 52

1 $84 \div 12 = 7$

2 In order: 3 5 6 6 6 6 7 7 8 10 10 10. The middle two numbers are 6 and 7, so the median is 6.5

3 There are four 6s, so 6 is the mode.

4 **C**: 10 − 3 = 7

Probability 54

1 $\frac{3}{5}$

2 **D**: $\frac{10}{30} = \frac{1}{3}$

3 $\frac{1}{6}$ of 24 = 4

2-D and 3-D shapes 58

1

2 **D**: the coloured pairs of edges in the diagram show where edges appear twice. Another way to do this is to count all the edges shown in the net (19) and subtract the number of edges on a cube (12), so 19 − 12 = 7

Angles 60

1 The known angles in the kite total 42° + 90° = 132°. All the angles in the kite must add up to 360°; that leaves 360° − 132° = 228°. Kites are symmetrical, so x must be the same size as the other unknown angle on the right. So x must be 228° ÷ 2 = 114°.

2 **C**: $\frac{1}{3}$ of a right angle is 30°, but e = 60°

Perimeter, area and volume 62

1 Volume of cuboid = length × width × height
= 15 × 10 × 8 = 150 × 8 = 1200mm^3.

There are 1000mm^3 in 1cm^3, so the answer is 1.2cm^3.

There are three different kinds of faces.

The top and base are each 15 × 10 = 150mm^2; total: 300mm^2. The left and right faces are each 10 × 8 = 80mm^2; total: 160mm^2. The front and back are each 15 × 8 = 120mm^2; total: 240mm^2.

Surface area = 300 + 160 + 240 = 700mm^2.

There are 100mm^2 in 1cm^2, so the answer is 7cm^2.

2 **A**: B and E have the same area.
A = 10 × 6 = 60cm^2 B = 15 × 5 = 75cm^2
C = $\frac{1}{2}$ × 8 × 12 = 48cm^2 D = 7^2 = 49cm^2
E = 10^2 − $\frac{1}{2}$ × 10 × 5 = 100 − 25 = 75cm^2

Coordinates 64

1 (1, 3)

2 **C**: (-4, 0) and (2, 3) are exactly two units above (-4, -2) and (2, 1), which are on the line.

Reflection, translation and rotation 66

1 (3, -1), (3, -5), (1, -5) and (1, -1)

2 **A**: the line of reflection has to pass through (2, 2) and slope diagonally down from left to right. Line E does this, but is too steep, so A is the correct answer.

Patterns and puzzles 68

1 The numbers of matchsticks needed is 9 (+14) 23 (+20) 43 (+26) 69. Each time, you increase by the same amount as before, plus 6: (14 + 6), (20 + 6), etc. So the answer is 69.

2 12 rectangles are required. This is one way to do it.

3 **B**: the first turn has to be L, so this rules out C. A and E don't reach square F. D does reach the square but goes over an oil patch. This leaves B.

Length, capacity and weight 72

1 **D**: the scale shows 1.4kg. Carol will add 0.8kg, so it will read 2.2kg afterwards.

2 Carlo's baby sister drinks 600ml of milk each day, which is 7 × 600ml = 4200ml of milk a week, or 4.2l.

3 320km = 40 × 8km = 40 × 5 miles = 200 miles.

Time 74

1 **B**: 4 hours + 12 hours = 16 hours

2 The total length is…
25 min + 1 hr 40 min + 5 min = 2 hr 10 min.
2 hr 10 min after 3.20pm is 5.30pm.

3 12 × 40 min = 480 min. 480 ÷ 60 = 8 hours.
8 × £3 = £24 altogether.

1   3700   3746 lies between 3700 and 3800 but is nearer to 3700. If less than 50 round down. If 50 or more round up.

2   **B**: Five units

Thousands	Hundreds	Tens	Units
2	6	1	5

3   36, 42   The rule is add 3.

4   7, 29   1 is not a prime number as it only has one factor.

5   72   The multiples of 6 are 6, 12, 18, 24, 30, 36, 42, 48, 54, 60, 66, **72**… and the multiples of 8 are 8, 16, 24, 32, 40, 48, 56, 64, **72**… so 72 is a common multiple of 6 and 8.

6   9   The factors of 18 are 2, 3 and 9 and the factors of 27 are 3 and 9 so 9 is the HCF.

7   4493   1000 + 3000 = 4000; 100 + 200 = 300; 80 + 60 + 40 = 180; 4 + 3 + 6 = 13   4000 + 300 + 180 + 13 = 4493

8   163   Use a number line and this SSFF rule: Start at the Second number and Finish at the First number.

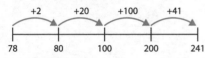

2 + 20 + 100 + 41 = 163

9   7°   Use a number line.

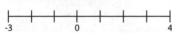

10   48

11   2   37 ÷ 5 = 7 remainder 2 or 5 × 7 = 35 and 35 + 2 = 37

12   121   484 ÷ 2 = 242 and 242 ÷ 2 = 121

13   £12.62   Approximate values to first find the total: 0.90 + 1.00 + 0.70 + 3.00 + 2.00 = 7.60 then subtract 22p (4p, 1p, 1p, 5p and 11p = 22p); 7.60 − 0.20 = 7.40 and 7.40 − 0.02 = £7.38

Then calculate the change: 7.38 + 0.02 = 7.40 + 0.60 = 8 and 8 + 12 = 20 so the change is 12 + 0.60 + 0.02 = £12.62

14   10   24 + 36 = 60 and 60 + 14 = 74 so 84 (total) − 74 = 10

15   9   You can use a 'number machine' to help you work this out.

$? \to \times 3 \to ? \to -7 \to 20$
$9 \leftarrow \div 3 \leftarrow 27 \leftarrow +7 \leftarrow 20$

Reverse the order and use inverse operations.

16   $x = 5$ Subtract 3 from both sides, so $3x = 15$ and divide both sides by 3, so $x = 5$

17   **D**:   convert all fractions to quarters: $\frac{1}{2} = \frac{2}{4}$; $\frac{4}{8} = \frac{2}{4}$; $\frac{3}{4} = \frac{3}{4}$; $\frac{5}{16} = \frac{1}{4} + \frac{1}{16}$; $\frac{3}{8} = \frac{1}{4} + \frac{1}{8}$. $\frac{1}{8}$ is larger than $\frac{1}{16}$ so $\frac{5}{16}$ is closest to $\frac{1}{4}$.

18   **B**:   find the equivalents: $\frac{1}{4} = \frac{9}{36}$; $\frac{1}{2} = \frac{18}{36}$; $\frac{4}{12} = \frac{12}{36}$. $\frac{1}{36} = \frac{1}{36}$; $\frac{3}{9} = \frac{12}{36}$. 18 is the largest numerator so the largest fraction is $\frac{1}{2}$.

19   $\frac{3}{4}$ $\frac{15}{20} = \frac{3}{4}$. Divide the numerator and the denominator by 5 (15 ÷ 5 = 3; 20 ÷ 5 = 4) to give the answer as a fraction in its lowest terms.

20   **C**: $\frac{2}{3} = \frac{4}{6} = \frac{6}{9}$

21   18.43   17.6 + 0.4 → 18 + 0.43 (0.83 − 0.4 = 0.43) → 18.43

22   14.6   3.8 + 0.2 → 4.0 + 14.0 → 18.0 + 0.4 → 18.4 and 14 + 0.40 + 0.20 = 14.6

23   0.75 $\frac{3}{4} = \frac{15}{20} = \frac{75}{100} = 0.75$ or $\frac{1}{4} = 0.25$ so $\frac{3}{4} = 0.25 \times 3 = 0.75$

24   **C**:   25% $= \frac{25}{100} \div 25 = \frac{1}{4}$

25   **B**:   1% of 250 $= \frac{250}{100}$ so 35% $= \frac{35 \times 250}{100}$

26   60% $\frac{15 \times 4}{25 \times 4} = \frac{60}{100}$

27   2 : 1   16 boys and 8 girls: ratio 16 : 8. Divide both 16 and 8 by 8 = 2 : 1

28   10 litres   180 ÷ 15 = 12km per litre so 120 ÷ 12 = 10 litres.

29   9   The second bar of the graph shows the result for apple.

30   30   7 + 9 + 3 + 6 + 5 = 30

31   **B**:   lowest is 3, highest is 9 so 9 − 3 = 6.

32   **C**:   the value that occurs most frequently in the list of data is 16. This is the mode.

A: 7 is the range; **B**:15 is the mean; **D**: 75 is the total.

33   **E**:   there are five factors of 12 in a set of ten cards numbered 1–10.

1, 2, 3, 4 and 6 are factors of 12.

$\frac{5}{10} = \frac{1}{2} = 50\%$.

34   **B**:   each number from 1 to 6 has an equal chance.

35   **D**:   all angles are the same size and all lengths are the same in a regular hexagon.

36   **B**:   A, C and E have no lines of symmetry, D has 6 lines of symmetry. A rectangle has 2 lines of symmetry.

37   **B**:   the angle is less than 45° (half a right angle – 90°) and more than 10°.

38   360

39   **D**:   7 + 4 + 7 + 4 = 22cm or 7 + 4 = 11 and 11 × 2 = 22cm

40   16cm²   Area of square = length × width: 4 × 4 = 16 (all sides of a square are equal).

41 (3, 7)   Always read across then up.

42 Check position of A (3, 7), B (3, 1), C (1, 1), D (1, 7). When you draw a line from A to B, B to C, C to D and D to A, you make a rectangle.

43

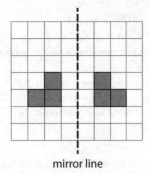

mirror line

44 The black shape is the translation of the original shape (the original shape has moved 3 squares to the right, 1 square down).

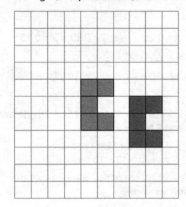

45

46 16 $1 + 3 + 5 + 7 = 16$

47 **B:**   a teaspoon could hold about 0.005 litres; a teacup could hold about 0.25 litres; a bath could hold about 50 litres; a swimming pool could hold about 350 000 litres. So the correct answer is that a washing up bowl could hold about 5 litres of water.

48 30 000mg   1000mg = 1g so $30 \times 1000 =$ 30 000mg

49 9.10am   08:45 + 15 minutes = 09:00 + 10 minutes = 09:10

50 **C:**   there are 30 days in the month of June.

1 30   Rounding to ten. Numbers ending in 5 round to the ten above.

2 100 002

3 56 64

4 131 $83 + 17 + 31 = 131$

5 117 $33 + 7 = 40; 40 + 10 = 50; 50 + 100 = 150; 7 + 10 + 100 = 117$

6 108 $36 \times 3 = 108$

7 16 $4000 \div 250 = 16$

8 125 $(11 \times 11) + (2 \times 2) = 125$

9 $y = 8$ $5 \times y = 40; 40 \div 5 = 8$ so $y = 8$

10 £8 $56 \div 7 = 8$

11 $\frac{5}{3}$ $1\frac{2}{3} = \frac{5}{3}$

12 8 $1.6 + 2.4 + 4 = 8$

13 60% $\frac{1}{5} \times 100 = 20$ so $\frac{3}{5}$ as a percentage is $20 \times 3 = 60\%$.

14 44% $100 - 56 = 44$

15 8   The ratio of red fish to green fish is 5 : 2 so if there are
             20 red fish there are four times as many. To find out the number
             of green fish the calculation is $4 \times 2 = 8$

16 2   2 is the mode as it is the number that occurs the most.

17 $\frac{9}{12}$ or $\frac{3}{4}$ Divide the blue balls by the total number of
                       balls to find the probability.

18 10   This is a 3-D shape with eight sides and two ends.

19 360°

20 20cm   A pentagon has five sides.
             $4 \times 5 = 20$

21 81cm² $9 \times 9 = 81$

22 12.35   (12.3 or 12.4 are acceptable answers)

23 21 litres $84 \div 4 = 21$

24 3000g $3 \times 1000 = 3000$

25 135min $60 + 60 + 15 = 135$

1. 240 — If less than 5 round down. If 5 or more round up.

2. D: Seven hundred

Thousands	Hundreds	Tens	Units
6	7	2	3

3. -6°C -4°C -3°C 0°C 3°C 4°C 5°C 7°C

4. 36 — $6 \times 6 = 36$ This is the square number series.

5. Triangular numbers

6. **B:** the multiples of 6 are 6, 12, 18, 24… and the multiples of 9 are 9, 18, 27… The answer is 18.

7. **A:** the factors of 57 are 1, 3, 19 and 57. The answer is 3.

8. 961 — $100 + 200 + 400 = 700$;

$90 + 20 + 60 + 70 = 240; 6 + 9 + 1 + 5 = 21$

$700 + 240 + 21 = 961$

9. 146 — $178 + 2 = 180; 180 + 20 = 200$;

$200 + 100 = 300; 300 + 24 = 24$

$100 + 24 + 20 + 2 = 146$

or $178 (+ 2) = 200 (+ 124) = 324$

and $22 + 124 = 146$

10. -3 °C

-5

11. **B:** $18 \times 18 \times 18 \times 18$

12. 13 — $10 \times 16 = 160; 208 - 160 = 48; 48 = 3 \times 16$ so $(10 + 3) \times 16 = 208$ or $13 \times 16 = 208$

13. 7 — $7 \times 7 = 49$

14. 51p — 5 pens cost 85 so 1 pen costs $85 \div 5 = 17$ and $3 \times 17 = 51p$

15. £54 — $482 - 50 = 432$ and $432 \div 8 = 54$

16. $p = 4$ — Substitute $r = 6$ and $s = 14$ into the formula to give $2p + 6 = 14$. Then subtract 6 from each side to give $2p = 8$. Then divide both sides by 2 to give $p = 4$

17. £30 — $20 \times 150 = 3000p$ and $3000 \div 100 = £30$

18. $\frac{15}{4}$ — 4 quarters make a whole. $3 \times 4 = 12$ so $3 = \frac{12}{4}$ and $3\frac{3}{4} = \frac{12}{4} + \frac{3}{4} = \frac{15}{4}$

19. 36 — $63 \div 7 = 9$ and $4 \times 9 = 36$

20. 42 — $\frac{1}{4}$ of $56 = 56 \div 4 = 14; \frac{3}{4}$ of $56 = 14 \times 3 = 42$

21. 12.56 — $4.86 + 0.04$ $4.90 + 0.10$ $5.00 + 12$ $17.00 + 0.42$ 17.42 and $12 + 0.42 + 0.1 + 0.04 = 12.56$

22. 0.306 — 0.31 0.47 0.5

23. $\frac{9}{20}$ — $\frac{45}{100} (\div 5) = \frac{9}{20}$

24. **E:** $0.18 \times 100 = 18\%$

25. 60% — $\frac{6}{10} \times 100 = 60\%$

26. 133 — 10% of $380 = 38$; $30\% = 38 \times 3 = 114$; $5\% = 38 \div 2 = 19$; $35\% = 114 + 19 = 133$

27. **A:** $10 \times 25000 = 250\,000$cm; $250\,000 \div 100 = 2500$m; $2500 \div 1000 = 2.5$km

28. 28 — $4 + 5 = 9; 63 \div 9 = 7; 7 \times 4 = 28$

There were 28 correct answers and 35 incorrect answers (28 : 35).

29. 4 pupils — There are 360°in a circle. $360 \div 60 = 6$ and $24 \div 6 = 4$ pupils.

30. 30° — Each pupil is represented by $360° \div 24 = 15°$ so 2 pupils $= 2 \times 15 = 30°$

31. 16.5 — the median is the middle value. 16.5 is halfway between 16 and 17 (12 15 16 16 16 17 17 18 19 19).

32. **C:** total number of lengths ÷ total number of people = mean. So $160 \div 10 = 16$ (A: 30 = range; B: 14 = median; D: 8 = mode; E: 160 = total).

33. **C:** between 1 and 7 there are four odd numbers (1, 3, 5 and 7) and three even numbers (2, 4 and 6), so the probability of landing on an odd number is four in seven.

34. $\frac{3}{8}$ — The total number of counters is $3 + 5 = 8$, so the probability of a white counter being taken out is three in eight.

35. **C:** Square

36. **B:** this shape can be cut out and folded to form a cube.

37. 125 ° — Angles in a full turn = 360° so all four angles must add up to 360. $360 - (105 + 45 + 85) = 125°$

38. 180°

39. 26cm — Missing measurements on shape are $6 - 3 = 3$ and $7 - 3 = 4$. Perimeter $= 6 + 3 + 3 + 4 + 3 + 7 = 26$

40. 140cm³ — $7 \times 4 \times 5 = 140$

41. **B:** 3 along to the right and 2 up from the origin, (3, 2).

42. (-4, -3) — 4 along to the left and 3 down from the origin.

43 Check position of R at (6, -3), 6 along to the right and 3 down from the origin.

44

A

45 **D:** path A leads you to 'J', not 'P'. Path B takes two wrong turns. Path C moves forward 10 spaces instead of 9 and path E takes one wrong turn, so D is the correct answer.

46 17 Number of squares increases by 3 each time.

Shape	1	2	3	4	5	6
Number of squares	2	5	8	11	14	17

47 **C:** 2.5 litres = 2500ml and 2500 ÷ 250 = 10

48 **E:** 8km = 5 miles so 1km is approximately $\frac{5}{8}$ mile and 5km = $5 \times \frac{5}{8} = \frac{25}{8}$

25 divided by 8 is approximately 3 so the answer is 3 miles.

49 14:35 (14.35 and 1435 accepted.)

50 16:35 (16.35 and 1635 accepted.)

15:55 + 5   16:00 +10 + 25   16:35

1 560 Rounding numbers to 10. Numbers ending in five always round up to the nearest 10.

2 1003

3 53 59 Prime numbers have only two factors; one and itself.

4 131 $87 + 13 + 31 = 131$

5 78 $5 + 8 = 23; 23 + 70 = 93; 8 + 70 = 78$

6 174 $87 \times 2 = 174$

7 108 $324 \div 3 = 108$

8 11 The square root of 49 is 7. The square root of 16 is 4, so $7 + 4 = 11$

9 $y = 6$ $6y + 2 = 38; 38 - 2 = 6y; 36 \div 6 = y$ so $y = 6$

10 £8 $32 \div 4 = 8$

11 22 $\frac{1}{3} \times 33 = 11$ so $\frac{2}{3}$ is $11 \times 2 = 22$

12 9.52 $1.62 + 2.9 + 5 = 9.52$

13 25% $\frac{5}{20} = \frac{1}{4}; \frac{1}{4} \times 100 = 25\%$

14 20cm $150\% = \frac{150}{100} = 1.5$, so $8 \times 1.5 = 12$ and $12 + 8 = 20$cm

15 6 The ratio of red apples to green apples is 7 : 2 so if there are 21 red apples there are three times as many. To find out the number of green apples the calculation is $3 \times 2 = 6$

16 3 All the repeated numbers should be counted; the median is middle value of an ordered set of numbers 1 2 2 2 **3** 3 6 7 9

17 $\frac{0}{13}$ Divide the number of white balls (there are none) by the total number of balls to find the probability.

18 14 A heptagon is a seven-sided shape. A heptagonal prism is a 3-D shape with seven sides and two ends. Therefore a heptagonal prism has 14 vertices (corners).

19 360°

20 56cm $7 \times 8 = 56$

21 121m² $11 \times 11 = 121$

22 166

23 2250ml $1000 + 1000 + 250 = 2250$

24 5600g $5.6 \times 1000 = 5600$

25 85mins $55 + 30 = 85$